☆ ☆

THE GAMBIT

A DEA Street Agent's Undercover Odyssey

BILL HEHR

BILL HEHR

☆ ☆

THE GAMBIT
A DEA Agent's Undercover Odyssey

This is a true story. All of the characters, names (other than those of informants two defendants and one agent), incidents, organizations, and dialogue are real, based on circuit court decisions and opinions, the authors, memory and Notes and the memories of other law enforcement officers consulted during the preparation of this book.

ISBN: 978-1-957883-20-5 Hardback
ISBN:978-1-957883-19-9 Paperback
ISBN: 978-1-957883-21-2 eBook
Library of Congress Control Number: 2024925407

Editing by Frank Sabina

Cover design by Dana Bree, StoneBear Design

Cover photo by Jodi Foucher

StoneBear Publishing LLC
Milford, PA 18337

www.stonebearpublishing.com

THE GAMBIT : A DEA AGENT'S UNDERCOVER ODYSSEY

☆ ☆

AWARDS AND HONORS

1975   Outstanding Contributions: DEA

1975   Special Achievement: DEA

1975   Special Achievement: DEA

1981   Commendation: IRS

1982   Outstanding Contributions: DEA

1983   Commendation: Wisconsin Narcotics Officer Association

1985   Sustained Superior Performance: DEA

1987   Excellence Of Performance: DEA

1991   Excellence Of Performance: DEA

1994   Dedication To Duty: IRS

1995   Distinguished Service: U.S. Dept Of Justice

1995   Proclamation: Making 9-22-95 Bill Hehr Day In Recognition of Contributions to Drug Law Enforcement In the City of Milwaukee

1999   Contributions to Law Enforcement: IRS

1999   Dedication To Duty: Louisiana State Police

ACKNOWLEDGMENTS

Thanks to my sister for making Mel an honest man and to my kids for their ideas about writing this book. Thanks to Augie, Mel, and Herb for being great partners and for always having my back. Thanks to Sharky, Oscar, "Harry" (you know who you are), Neil, The U.S. Attorney's Office for the Eastern District of Wisconsin and the Milwaukee Police Department vice squad and the 700 tactical units. Finally, to all of the DEA employees and law enforcement officers who were taken from us while fighting the fight.

A special thanks to my parents for the many sleepless nights about which they endured but never complained.

DEDICATION

This book is dedicated to Jeanne whose patience, support, selflessness, and love has made it possible.

DISCLAIMER

This book explores historical drug convictions that occurred 30 to 40 years ago to shed light on societal and systematic issues of that era. All information presented is based on publicly available records, recollections, and notes and is included for educational, journalistic, and historical purposes

Every effort has been made to ensure the accuracy of the information presented in this book however due to the passage of time memory limitations and potential discrepancies in public records some inaccuracies may exist readers are encouraged to verify any statements or claims through primary sources where necessary.

The inclusion of individuals, names and details of their convictions is not intended to defame, harass, or harm those named. This book's goal is to contribute to public understanding of historical drug policies, their enforcement and their impacts. The focus is on providing context for the systematic challenges and societal effects of those convictions.

The author acknowledges that individuals named in this book may have since rehabilitated or undergone significant life changes. This book aims to document historical events and they're significance, not to define or judge individuals solely by their past actions. The intention is to emphasize the broader societal and historical implications of these events.

Under US law information from public records may be lawfully disclosed. Nevertheless this book respects individual privacy to

☆ ☆

the extent possible while maintaining historical accuracy and public interest. The names of two dealers, one informant, and one agent have been changed for security reasons. Some of the drug deals referred to do not include the names of the dealers. That is only because those investigations were very short term and for the most part conducted in parts of the United States other than Milwaukee making the retrieval of records more difficult.

Some people are referred to only by first names and that's only because records could not be located completely identifying them. Lastly sometimes convictions of individuals are not mentioned and again that's because records could not be located.

TESTIMONIALS

"While a detective in the 1990s. I had the fortunate opportunity to be assigned to a Federal Drug Enforcement Task Force. During this assignment, Agent Hehr supervised our task force leading to the arrests of individuals responsible for hundreds of kilos of cocaine. The investigative techniques used by agent Hehr were cutting edge, such as aerial surveillance, consensual knock and talks, wiretaps, and search warrants. Special Agent Hehr was an expert in narcotics investigations whose skills were apart from many others."

– **Oscar Perez,** Retired Deputy Inspector,
Milwaukee Police Department

"A retired Law Enforcement Officer, I have 31 years of police experience, including undercover work, SWAT/K-9, and investigations. I found it a very good read. I get the first chapter or two as a groundwork on the explosion of drugs in the U.S. and more specifically in Milwaukee where I was "on-the-job". It was fast-paced and informative. I often felt my adrenalin pumping as I read. I think both law enforcement personnel and, perhaps lawyers will find it informative as well as anyone who has a general interest in law enforcement and the workings of DEA agents and police officers and the dangers that they face to keep us safe."

– **Jim Sanfilippo**, Milwaukee Police Department, Retired

"Hehr is able to bring the reader onto the drug-ridden streets of Chicago and Milwaukee with description that makes the reader sit back and wonder how any of the men and women survived the dangers that awaited them as they attempted to rid the cities of the underworld of the illicit drug business. He is able to make the reader take a deep breath in anticipation of what will happen during a drug operation, and a moment later have you smiling at some of the antics of the agents and drug dealers. As a retired DEA Special Agent, I appreciate Hehr's candor and ability to bring the DEA undercover agents' job to light."

– **David Hess,** DEA Group Supervisor, retired,
author of *Ambush* and *Gamble*

☆ ☆

TABLE OF CONTENTS

Awards and Honors. iv
Acknowledgments .v
Dedication. v
Disclaimer vi
Testimonials viii

1.	Milwaukee, Early 1990s. 1
2.	How It Began 14
3.	Background 20
4.	Enter Cocaine 27
5.	The First Years 29
6.	Deep Cover 33
7.	More Undercover 42
8.	Climbing the Ladder 49
9.	Transfer to Milwaukee 54
10.	CENTAC 4 62
11.	Side Story. 68
12.	Tip of the Spear 70
13.	New Sheriff In Town 73
14.	Keep On Moving 75
15.	You Can't Make This Stuff Up 79
16.	The Birth of the Cartels and Their Impact On Middle America 83
17.	Not Just a Regular Flight 89
18.	Moving On. 93
19.	Witness/Informant/Drug Dealer 105
20.	Moving Back to the Racine Case 112
21.	The Surveillance From Hell 115
22.	Summer, 1982 123
23.	The Case Takes a Turn 129
24.	Too Close For Comfort 134
25.	Another Close Call 137

26. Mel 141
27. Mel, The Preacher, and I 147
28. Michigan Bikers 152
29. More Michigan 156
30. You Meet People In the Strangest Places 160
31. One More Fishing Trip 165
32. Skag, Horse, Junk, Smel, H, White, Black Tar,
    Chiva, Boy, Brown. 168
33. A Little More Heroin 171
34. Heroin Backstory 175
35. Reverse Undercover Deal. 177
36. Texas Dealers 182
37. New Agent In the Office 186
38. Keep Moving Forward 188
39. Iran Contras In Milwaukee? 200
40. Sad Goodbye. 208
41. More Sorrow. 210
42. No Words Could Describe The Depravity 213
43. Miami Calls For Help 217
44. I Get Burned 222
45. The Milwaukee Street Gang 224
46. Expert Testimony 241
47. Side Job. 242
48. A New Technique and Two New Partners 247
49. Monday Morning Texas Car 251
50. Another Monday Morning Meeting Missed 254
51. Another Bingo. 257
52. Just Another Monday. 260
53. One Last Milwaukee Conversation 263
54. Another Airplane Ride 265
55. New Orleans 269
56. Strike Three 271
57. The Transition 273
About the Author 276

U.S. Court of Appeals, 7th Circuit, 1 F. 3d 644 (7th Cir 1993)

"We hold that the District Court addressed the concerns the panel expressed in Duarte One. First, it is undisputed that agent Hehr has 20 years of experience investigating, analyzing, and testifying concerning drug operations such as the one directed by Duarte. An educated professional, his formal training with the DEA has been supplemented, if not exceeded, by his training and experience on the streets during the course of hundreds of undercover assignments and thousands of interviews of drug suspects. His record as far as we can discern, is unblemished. He testified in this case solely in his capacity as an expert witness who had no involvement whatsoever in the particular investigations that led to the defendant's arrest."

1

Milwaukee, Early 1990s

The cold industrial heartbeat of Milwaukee pulsed around me as I drove the shadowy streets. I loved the sights and smells of the early morning city. It was only during that time when the city seemed civilized. I had experienced the feelings on dozens of occasions. Each time was different, and yet seemed to be the same—different neighborhoods, different drug dealers, different circumstances, but with the same feelings of anticipation that surged an adrenaline rush, and sometimes sadness. I had witnessed a lot of things –bad things–on those same streets, the streets that seemed so peaceful in the morning. My instincts were razor sharp, honed by the two decades of my undercover work. I had seen the underbelly of the drug world up close, and tonight would be no different. During the quiet solitude of an early morning, I had a chance to reflect on a drug deal, recently completed.

THE NEW INFORMANT

On this evening as the clock ticked toward 5 p.m., my fellow agents and I were winding down the end of a long day, sharing the usual end of shift banter. But the relaxed mood in the squad

bay was abruptly shattered when my phone rang with an urgent call from a reliable informant known for delivering golden tips. The informant indicated that he had just left a house and had observed about a half pound of cocaine. He also described the guy who was in possession of the cocaine as being on a two-day relentless high.

Not being one to pass up a sure thing, I called an assistant United States Attorney, and together they feverishly drafted a search warrant affidavit. However, the biggest challenge would be getting the search warrant approved by a federal magistrate who understandably wasn't thrilled to be disturbed just before cocktail hour. The magistrate's grumbling was barely a whisper against the backdrop of our urgency. Even federal magistrates have cocktail hours!

Warrant in hand, I quickly devised a strategy for breaching the target residence and set off to lay low for a surveillance operation before hitting the house. After about two hours of no activity, I decided to hit the house and the plan was executed, catching the drug dealer completely off guard. However, my team was caught off guard when we kicked the door down and saw the dealer lying on the floor in the living room seemingly comatose. The team's adrenaline was surging as they quickly secured the premises.

While the rest of the residence was being cleared, one of the more compassionate agents on the raid team began questioning the dealer who managed to croak out a desperate plea for water. His parched voice was a grim reminder of the dire state he was in, exacerbated by the pile of cocaine languishing beside him.

This agent who began the dealer's interview reached for a dog's bowl half filled with dog food and passed it to me. "How about cleaning this up and getting some water?" While rolling

my eyes, I dutifully filled it, setting it on the floor next to the dealer. "Anything else?" I sarcastically muttered while walking away. The dealer then rolled over with a little help from the compassionate agent and with a mix of disorientation and desperation, he began lapping the water out of the bowl just as a dog would do. The owner's small dog, who also must have been dying of thirst, ran for the bowl of water and fought for whatever water was remaining.

What l didn't realize was that this guy drinking water would soon become an informant who was willing to give up his Florida sources of supply for cocaine. The same guy was strong enough with his Florida people that he could introduce me as a potential buyer of a large quantity of cocaine. Over the next couple of days, the guy who was lying on the floor became an informant.

I was going to make a decision during the upcoming undercover negotiations with two Colombian cocaine dealers that placed me and others in jeopardy. As a result of this decision and upon a lot of reflection, I put almost 20 years of undercover work to rest and found a new way to slow down drug traffickers and their organizations. Prior to this undercover endeavor, my philosophy had always been safety first with the agents that I worked with or police officers I taught or worked with.

THE REVELATION

The informant provided valuable intel, phone numbers, and past dealings. I spent weeks debriefing him, cross-referencing information with the Miami DEA, and laying the groundwork for an undercover operation. The informant was proven to be reliable, and the Colombians, Jesus and Chepe, were the real deal. My mind raced with possibilities. Through a series of

carefully orchestrated calls, the informant introduced me as his affluent friend looking to purchase large quantities of cocaine. Jesus and Chepe were gradually convinced by the informant's cover story. They had made successful transactions in the past on many occasions, and I seemed like another lucrative opportunity where everybody could make money.

THE COLOMBIANS

The informant had been in regular contact with the two Colombians. I had the informant start laying a foundation for my introduction to them. Over a period of several weeks the informant casually mentioned to Jesus, one of the Columbians, that he had a guy, that being me, with a ton of money. The Colombians readily accepted the informant's cover story along with background information on the informant's money guy.

On prior occasions the informant sent guys to Miami to purchase cocaine from these Colombians, Jesus and Chepe. Up until this point all the transactions were successful and the informant, Jesus, Chepe, and the customers all made money. There was no reason other than normal paranoia for the Colombians to be concerned about me.

THE NEGOTIATIONS

I thought that I was in a perfect position to have the informant place a recorded phone call to the Colombians and introduce me on the phone as his longtime friend who was looking for kilogram quantities of cocaine. During the call the Colombians weren't interested in talking to me.

On one of the subsequent recorded calls to the Colombians, they asked the informant if he was ready for another load of

cocaine based on the informant's confidence that sooner or later, they would talk to me who was present during this call. The informant said he was in good shape and didn't need any additional cocaine.

He continued by asking the Colombians if he should ask me whether I wanted more cocaine. After some back and forth with the Colombians, who preferred only to deal with the informant, the Colombians asked how much cocaine I would be interested in. The informant told them he would call them back after talking to me. As I listened intently to this conversation, I became convinced that this could be a real deal.

The informant and I discussed what amount of cocaine would not spook the Colombians, and it was decided that five kilos would be a good number that shouldn't arouse any suspicion based on the informant's prior business dealings. Additionally, the informant had mentioned my name enough times by now that the Colombians' guard was down considerably, thinking that I was the real thing.

The informant again placed a recorded call to the Colombians and indicated that I would be interested in five kilos but wanted to make sure I got a decent price. After some haggling between the informant and the Colombians, I seized the moment and hollered loud enough for the Colombians to be able to hear on their end of the phone, "Fuck this! Let me talk to them" and grabbed the phone.

I began. "What's the problem? This shit is getting old!"

One of the Columbians responded, "No problem, just confusion."

"No need for confusion, I got the ching and you got the chang."

"Ok, Ok. We need to think about it!"

"Ok but time's wasting, and I got people who are pushing. And I don't like being pushed!"

"*Si*, just give us some time to figure this out. We will be in touch!"

"Yeah. Ok, but no more stalling." Then I heard the click on the other line.

The Colombians were intrigued but cautious. They needed time to think. I knew that they didn't need time to think; they needed to get together with their cocaine source supply and get his approval for the five kilos before the deal could proceed. This of course threw a possible wrench in the deal but also provided an opportunity to climb one step higher on the ladder.

MIAMI RENDEZVOUS

A couple days later the informant received a phone call from Jesus who indicated that they would deal with me directly, but the transaction would have to occur on their turf. I agreed, setting the stage for a high stakes encounter. I told the informant to tell them I was fine with that and that I could be in Miami within two days. A series of phone calls occurred between the informant and Jesus during which time it was decided that I would meet the Colombians at a specific airport hotel on Friday evening. Physical descriptions were exchanged, and a price was settled upon. All conversations recorded as routine practice.

I contacted a Miami DEA group and briefed them about the proposed plans.

The plan was simple yet fraught with risk: meet at a hotel, see the cocaine, give the arrest signal, and wrap it up. Even though I was confident in my undercover capabilities, I knew there may be changes to the plan in the middle of negotiations.

Plans were made with the surveillance agents including how

much latitude I had after I met the Colombians—a lot harder to say than to do. My confidence overpowered my common sense when it came right down to it.

MEETING THE COLOMBIANS

Finally, it was game time, and the surveillance agents were all in place when two Colombians matching the description previously provided entered the hotel lobby and joined me at a sofa in the airport hotel lobby. I felt a familiar surge of adrenaline.

I spent about 20 minutes with the Colombians negotiating face-to-face in the lobby on how the transaction would proceed, trying to keep the operation within the safe bounds of the plan. The Colombians insisted that the five kilos were just minutes away, and that it would require a short drive to retrieve them.

As hard as I could, I tried to get the Colombians to just go and get the coke and bring it back to the lobby. However, the harder I tried, the Colombians became more stubborn and said that was the only way the deal could go. At this point I figured that the Colombians wanted to make a heat run to see if they were being followed by the police.

One of the Columbians spoke. "You don't understand, Gringo. Your only option is to take a cab to the airport and go back to Milwaukee."

I responded, "What you don't understand, Señor, is that no gringo in Milwaukee would be stupid enough to come to Miami to try to cop five kilos from two Colombians he had never met before expecting to return to Milwaukee in one piece."

"You've got a very good point there, but that doesn't change anything. You either take a ride to get the coke or bye," they answered while laughing.

"How long of a ride is it going to be?"

"Less than five minutes, and if it's anymore, just get out of the car and walk back."

Having a feeling in my gut that I had had so many times before, I felt that this was a legitimate deal, and that they were going to just take a short drive to identify any surveillance that might be following. If the Colombians did pick up surveillance before the transaction, they would probably just throw me out of the car and say bye.

CHANGE IN THE PLAN

I had total confidence in the surveillance abilities of the Miami group of agents and decided to roll the dice and take a ride. Roll the dice and take a ride? Not only was that an extremely dangerous move, but it also violated the agreement I made with the Miami DEA as to how the deal was supposed to play out. Expecting a surveillance team to be able to do an adequate job when a way-too-confident undercover agent altered the plan was flat out dangerous.

By altering the plan, I put the surveillance team in a very precarious situation. Of course, the first job of a surveillance team was to protect the undercover agent and make sure he got home at night. When I decided to take a ride with the two Colombians, the surveillance team very well could have thought that I was being kidnapped and would therefore have to intervene with guns drawn. There was of course a distress signal that I would have given the surveillance team had that occurred.

If the surveillance team didn't come to that conclusion and believed that the two Colombians and I were going to get the cocaine, they would have to make sure that they followed the Colombians close enough but not too close. Following them too closely could bring heat on the deal. But then again, following

them not close enough would jeopardize losing the undercover agent. All these thoughts raced through my mind as I was trying to decide if I should take a ride with the Colombians.

Violating everything I had taught and practiced, I agreed with the two Colombians to get in their car and drive to where the five kilos of cocaine were allegedly being stashed. A very risky deviation from the plan. The Miami DEA surveillance team would scramble to adapt, their primary goal now was to ensure my safety.

I knew the Miami surveillance team that was covering me would be incensed that I broke protocol. I wasn't looking for trouble but may have found it. Although the Miami surveillance team was prepared for all circumstances, they were not completely prepared for me to deviate so radically from the approved plan.

THE RIDE

While still waiting in the hotel lobby, one of the Colombians left and picked up the car. I jumped in the back seat with the two Colombians in the front seat, Jesus driving. While trying to be inconspicuous, I was surreptitiously scanning, looking for surveillance vehicles who were hopefully following, but saw none.

Within a mile or two of the airport hotel, the driver pulled into an underground parking lot that was vacant except for one car. The tension in the car was palpable. The driver parked the car next to the only car left in the parking lot. It makes sense since it was Friday night. Or maybe there were more Colombians in that car lying in wait. The parking garage was dark with a musty smell, and I had a difficult time adjusting my eyes to the darker setting.

I scanned the area quickly for any other bad guys and tried to absorb everything surrounding me that could be used in case

things got really bad. Previously I had conducted a pretty good look at the Columbians while in the hotel and didn't notice any obvious signs they were carrying weapons. I also formulated a plan if I had to shoot, where I would shoot from, and what barricade I could possibly use–the posts in the garage or one of the two cars. Not many options and close quarters. This all occurred within a millisecond after pulling into the garage.

The Colombians and I got out of the car at which time I took a full grip on the Smith & Wesson. I didn't try to hide the fact that I was armed since I already lost control of the deal which was something I taught thousands of policemen never to do. The Colombians couldn't help but notice me squeezing my weapon. Chepe added, "That won't be necessary."

While I was still scanning the area, Chepe went to the car they parked next to and opened the trunk. As he was opening a trunk, I thought that it was game time. There would either be cocaine in the trunk or an extra Colombian. At this point I was getting ready for the worst-case scenario and was preparing myself for some real drama. *Why in the heck did I get myself in this situation!!!!*

I had my course of action mapped out with my eyes darting between my potential adversaries and surroundings. As the Colombian popped open the trunk, I saw a black plastic bag. With a mixture of apprehension and anticipation, I took a step back, relief mingled with the ever-present danger. One of the Colombians said go ahead and look. I carefully peeled back the layers of clothes in the bag, trying to watch the Colombians at the same time.

I was relieved to see that the black plastic bag contained five book-sized packages which looked like familiar wrappings containing kilograms of cocaine. God bless duct tape and God

bless the telltale smell of ether that remained in the trunk. Ether was a primary precursor for the manufacturer of cocaine, and duct tape was used to securely wrap the kilogram packages.

Still in a state of heightened awareness, I insisted that the Columbians would have to bring the cocaine to the lobby of the hotel where we first met. That's where the transfer of money and drugs would occur. They had previously determined a price so that was off the table and now the haggling began as to where they were going to bring the cocaine. Were they going to bring the cocaine to me in the lobby, or will I go to bring the money to them? *And shit, drive the damn car!!!!*

I certainly wasn't out of the woods yet and told the Columbians that the deal was going to occur in the hotel lobby, or it wasn't going to occur at all. At that point I was done with the intensity of the deal and wouldn't have it any other way because I had regained control of the deal, hopefully.

After moving from the car containing the cocaine, I jumped in the original car with Jesus driving. Chepe drove the car with five kilos in it. On the way back to the hotel, I again did not see any surveillance and was still devising plans for how I would get out of this situation. I got out of the original car and met Chepe who was in the coke car and in the process of getting the plastic bag out of his trunk.

Chepe retrieved the plastic bag and opened the rear driver's side door, placing the plastic bag in a satchel. Chepe walked with me into the hotel. The plan was for me to go to my room and retrieve the money. Chepe didn't waste any time at all loading the coke into the satchel and walking into the lobby. The tide had turned.

THE ARREST

I was totally confident I would have surveillance in the lobby. As I entered the hotel, the first thing I saw was two guys from the group who were supporting me and then some other agents just wandering around.

I told the Columbians to have a seat in some chairs in the middle of the lobby and that I would call my room and have the money delivered to the lobby.

As I was walking away, I gave a prearranged arrest signal and out of nowhere a half a dozen more agents appeared and placed the Columbians under arrest. It was a textbook arrest, speed, surprise and precision.

Surveillance had been maintained outside of the hotel and observed the original car with Jesus pulling away. When they received the arrest sign, they pulled over and arrested the driver of the original car. Neither of the Colombians resisted or were armed although a small caliber handgun was located under the driver's seat. The Miami agents executed the arrests with speed and precision. It was very impressive watching them in action, and I could tell that they had worked as a group on many similar arrests.

POST ARREST "SPANKING"

I deviated from the game plan because my gut told me it was going to be a legitimate deal, and I went with my gut. Although ultimately my gut was right, I still should not have deviated from the plans I made with the Miami agents.

They gave up a Friday night to help some hump from Milwaukee get five kilos which to them was nothing but a drop in the bucket. Hopefully either Jesus or Chepe would decide to

work with the Miami DEA instead of going to prison. I didn't find out about the outcome of their case. After I gave the arrest signal and determined all was well, the Miami guys handled the rest. I then returned to Milwaukee to something less than a hero's welcome.

Upon my return, I had a closed-door session with my boss, affectionately nicknamed Old Paint, who indicated that Miami had called Chicago (Milwaukee reported to Chicago), and Chicago had called my boss and directed that I receive a severe spanking for what I did in Miami. It wasn't quite that harmless. My boss said, "Don't ever pull that crap again!" He went on to say, "Nice job, Bill, now go make a case!" I walked out the door with my tail tucked between my legs.

When I became a supervisor, I adopted the same philosophy and always told my guys, "I'll have your back, but you first have to be safe and make cases." The truth of the matter was that DEA agents very seldom must be pushed to work and go out and make cases because it's almost a genetic thing. Agents just do it.

I also learned a great lesson during the above deal. This specific deal taught me that the line between trusting my gut and wanting the deal to be successful was very hazy. On the Miami deal, my gut was telling me that it was a real deal and to go for it. I went for it, and it turned out okay. But it also turned out to be a humbling experience.

2
How It Began

Over a span of 28 years, I served as a Special Agent with the Bureau of Narcotics and Dangerous Drugs and the Drug Enforcement Administration. From the grimy streets of the Chicago Divisional office to the hustle and bustle of the Milwaukee resident office, and the laid-back vibe of the New Orleans divisional office, I found himself swiftly immersed in the chaotic life of a BNDD/DEA agent. This journey provided me not just a job but a rewarding and sometimes perilous life experience.

My experiences and those of other agents and officers who have worked extensively undercover, underscores the inherent danger of drug law enforcement operations. Although becoming more and more confident working undercover I was always mindful of the dangers involved. My confidence caused me to let my guard down on one occasion which easily could have ended in disaster. Danger came in many forms and sometimes, unfortunately, it was recognized too late.

I basically never knew until I knew.

Embarking on street-level operations is akin to climbing a ladder starting from the bottom rungs and striving to reach the top. My aspiration was to trace the drug supply chain from buying small amounts of drugs in Milwaukee to targeting the

ultimate domestic sources in cities like Miami, San Diego or Los Angeles. Miami, being a primary source city for much of the Eastern United States, represented the top of the ladder.

In the long run that was ultimately the objective of offices like the Milwaukee office. They would start by initiating investigations at the street level, gathering evidence, making an arrest, cultivating informants, and gradually working up the chain to disrupt major drug trafficking networks often leading to operations in cities like Miami.

I was able to work undercover for a period of 23 years on hundreds of cases, many of which were successful, some of which were not. I was fortunate enough to walk away from undercover work physically unscathed. Unexpectedly, about seven years after my retirement, I experienced a period of nightmares, mostly about getting cornered in dangerous situations with bad guys who were always 'chasing.'

I started jumping out of bed trying to escape them and ended up with a few minor injuries, including a fractured skull and various bumps and bruises. Although I slept sound as a baby while I was on the job, something must have been tucked deep inside waiting for the right time to be released. I really did see stars when the top of my head met concrete after diving headfirst out of a California king size bed!

Some of the cases I worked on put me in situations that upon reflection were funny, ironic and almost always nerve-wracking. My experiences provided a glimpse of what it was like to work with informants, go undercover, conduct surveillance, and participate in buy-busts on a routine basis. (A buy-bust is an investigation where an undercover agent has no intentions of purchasing the drugs but arresting the dealer once the drugs were observed by the undercover agent.)

Additionally, I was involved in many cases that did not involve undercover work but involved investigation and interviewing witnesses as opposed to working undercover. And there were cases that I worked on that involved a mixture of working undercover and developing information for more complex conspiracy cases.

The trafficker located in cities like Milwaukee and New Orleans who were the sources of supply for those cities, the desperate street trafficker located in all cities or the international trafficker who was dealing with thousands of kilos of cocaine and millions of dollars all had the potential for violence.

It was the agent's job who was working on these cases to create a scenario that was the safest possible course of action. Sometimes if an agent did a perfect job evaluating the informant, it still wasn't good enough. Some informants were so good at being scumbags that they slipped under the radar. What I learned for sure was that working undercover on a routine basis was not for the timid. I happened to begin my career at a time when a huge transition was occurring with both drug dealers and drug agents.

In the tumultuous decades of the 1970s and 1980s, a seismic shift reshaped the very fabric of American drug culture. Not only did the nation's craving for illegal drugs undergo a profound transformation, but the mechanisms of enforcing drug laws also experienced a radical evolution. This transformation in the American desire for illicit substances was fueled with the introduction of quantities of cocaine and marijuana that had not been seen before. The amount of money generated through the sales of cocaine and marijuana surpassed the budgets of many countries.

Enterprising criminals from Colombia, Bolivia, and Peru

orchestrated intricate operations to cultivate the coca plant. Following this, they meticulously processed the plant into cocaine base, culminating in the conversion of cocaine base to the infamous cocaine hydrochloride. Responding to this new threat, forward thinkers at The Drug Enforcement Administration created a unit of elite specially trained DEA agents who attacked the problem in the source countries.

The web of transportation routes for this potent product, cocaine hydrochloride, mutated into complex schemes involving airplanes, seagoing vessels, vehicles, and human smugglers. The sheer scale and audacity of these trafficking networks reached unprecedented levels, creating danger and intrigue across continents. The victims of the scheme too often were drug agents killed directly by the dealers and innocent citizens who caught in the crossfire. Of course, many drug dealers met their creator and were currently serving very hard time.

The colossal profits reaped by the Colombians alone soared into the realm of billions of dollars. This staggering financial windfall not only fueled the insidious trade but also heightened the stakes in the ongoing battle between law enforcement and drug empires. My immersion into the crucible of this era, where the clash between supply and demand reached a fever pitch, caused me to witness the American drug culture forever altered. The 1970s and 1980s stood as a testament to the always changing war between illicit appetites, criminal ingenuity, and the relentless pursuit of enforcement.

In 1970, Congress unleashed a new tool in the war against drug distribution with the passage of the Comprehensive Drug Abuse Prevention and Control Act, coupled with the Controlled Substances Act. Tucked within the latter was 21 USC 846, better known as The Conspiracy Law.

This game-changing legislation declared it a criminal act for individuals to conspire with others in plotting a drug-related crime, be it smuggling or distribution. It empowered law enforcement to bring the hammer down, not just when the crime went down, but even if an agreement was struck between two or more individuals to embark on a drug-trafficking escapade. The fight against drugs just got a whole lot fiercer!"

The vast quantities of cocaine and marijuana, combined with the game-changing passage of the Controlled Substances Act, thrust society into the gamble of immense profits and unprecedented risks. The aftermath: murder rates soaring, colossal organizations— menacing gangs—all rising from the streets of America.

Rewind to the eve of July 1, 1973, when the federal government's anti-drug force, previously known as The Bureau of Narcotics and Dangerous Drugs (BNDD), was at the forefront.

Recognizing the intensifying drug crisis, President Nixon orchestrated an organizational shift—the inception of The Drug Enforcement Administration (DEA). This agency, a joining of the BNDD and around 1400 United States customs agents, was at the time considered a super agency.

The merger dictated that 1400 customs agents, who had no training in the work conducted by BNDD, directed them to report to the new agency, DEA. Although most of the customs agents who transferred to BNDD were good, hard-working agents, there were a lot of bumps in the road, and it took a long time for the customs agents to become effective drug enforcement agents.

The main problem with the merger was that the customs agents had little or no training in undercover work, which all BNDD agents had, and in fact performed on a daily basis. Surveillance was another skill set that the BNDD agents were trained on and executed daily. Most of the problems seemed to resolve themselves once BNDD agents peeled the skin of the customs agents and found out that they both had the same goals and needed to work together. It didn't take long, notwithstanding a few bumps in the road for the customs agents and the now DEA agents working together. Over a period of about six months, the customs agents slowly began to assimilate into the existing BNDD enforcement groups and became an integral part of each group. Some agents became excellent undercover agents, and some agents became excellent surveillance agents. Ultimately, both the BNDD and customs agents began working together as one agency with one mission, DEA.

It was somewhat of a cultural war between two different groups of men and women who had different cultural philosophies. Ultimately, the wrinkles were ironed out over a period, and DEA became an adversary drug traffickers wanted to avoid at all costs! The clash of philosophies, the challenges faced, the difference of enforcement philosophies made the war on drugs even more difficult, at least in the beginning

3

Background

Although as time moved on, I became much more adept at working undercover and being able to figure out the little cues that the drug dealer would subconsciously send during deals. I was always mindful of the dangers involved. This could be the danger presented by the trafficker or it could be a conspirator of the drug dealer hiding in the shadows out of sight. We basically never knew until we knew . . .

In the dynamic realm of Federal Drug law enforcement, I was an active participant. Sometimes too active for my own good. I loved the job and the work. I made hundreds of undercover purchases, interviewed thousands of witnesses and informants, conducted a myriad of surveillance, and was the go-to expert witness, testifying as an expert witness in dozens of cases over a period of 10 years. I was the only expert drug witness that had been qualified to testify in Wisconsin. My experiences and those of other agents in offices who have worked extensive undercover assignments highlight the dangers involved in undercover drug law enforcement.

The expert saw what drug notes meant because almost invariably the notes were unique to the drug dealer but always

meant the same thing. Drug notes typically reflected who owed how much for a specific quantity of drugs and the price for those drugs. Also, they reflected what the dealer owed to his sources of supply. The names on the drug notes were almost always nicknames or abbreviations for the real person.

The reason dealers weren't more straightforward was because they didn't want the police to interpret their misdeeds. The jargon used by drug dealers was unique when they spoke to each other. An expert could decipher the code words used during telephone calls that were being recorded by a wiretap. The telephone numbers called by a drug dealer to his customers or sources of supply required an expert to explain how phone calls typically identified the structure of an organization. The numbers were revealed after the drug dealer's phone records were subpoenaed.

STREET REP

Notwithstanding, my greatest strength was an unblemished reputation which gave strength to my relationships with defendants, defense attorneys, prosecuting attorneys, magistrates and judges. I also developed a reputation on the street, causing more than one dealer to hire an attorney and work out a plea agreement after I confronted the dealer and threatened to open an investigation on him. Offering little tidbits of evidence that I was confident of, were used as the basis for plea negotiations and reduced penalties.

This technique worked because my reputation among the defense bar was solid. I contacted defense attorneys and told them that I was looking at their client and now was the time to jump on board. When they didn't, the hammer usually dropped a lot harder than if they would have cooperated.

In today's world of hyper paranoia, I probably would not have survived because of the personal relationships I developed with several criminal defense attorneys. Never crossing the line or even thinking about that, I followed the lead of a veteran Milwaukee Police Department detective who told me which attorneys he could trust and which attorneys he couldn't trust. One of the attorneys, a premier criminal defense attorney in the Midwest and one who caused DEA chemists' ulcers, became close friends with both my wife Jeanne and me.

Knowing that DEA agents often worked late at night, this attorney allowed me and whoever I may be working with access to a garage refrigerator which was full of beer. Several other DEA agents and I attended the 50th, 60th, and 70th birthday parties for this particular attorney. Even a DEA chemist from Chicago whom the attorney routinely used as a whipping board showed up and had a good time.

One day the office secretary answered a call. "Could I speak to Special Agent Hehr?"

"Could I ask who's calling?" the secretary responded.

"No, he'll know."

I took the call. "Where, What time?"

"The place off Mason St, 6:30, And please don't get all dressed up for the occasion." (Sarcasm related to getting dressed up)

"Bye."

"Don't be late. I'm important."

And so, it went every couple of weeks over a period of about 20 years. We never talked about past or pending cases but did talk a lot about criminal law, conspiracy law, jury selection, cross examination and on and on. I learned enough about criminal law from these 'meetings' that I could have hung out a shingle. And that's the rest of the story . . .

☆ ☆

There were other attorneys that I would frequently meet after a trial or a hearing at a local Irish pub and throw back a few beers. On one occasion on a Sunday afternoon, I got a call at my home from a sitting federal judge who asked if I would be available to come to the judge's home as soon as possible because of a possible problem. I complied and immediately drove to the fashionable home of the judge who explained that he had just purchased this house and after the purchase found out that it was once owned by a drug trafficker. Additionally, the judge explained that there were suspicious weeds growing in this backyard next to the garage and wondered if I would be willing to look at them. I looked along with the judge and his wife and confirmed the judge's worst suspicion. Indeed, they were marijuana plants which I then picked by the roots, stuffed in my government car, and drove to a field near my home where they were disposed of, never to be mentioned again. Yes, indeed, those were different days!

After several years, starting in the late 1970s, I became part of the Chicago divisional training team which was responsible for conducting training in Wisconsin, Illinois, Indiana, Minnesota and North Dakota. I took my experiences on the street and transferred them as best I could to the thousands of state and local police officers that were in attendance. Surveillance, undercover, and informant handling were my primary areas of responsibility. It was a pleasant distraction from the grind of the street, and I loved working with state and local policemen to hone their talents. During the DEA state and local schools, which were two weeks long, two themes resonated as primary doctrine: The power of a good informant and safety. If you had a good informant, you could be Frankie G Duck, and the bad guy would sell cocaine to Frankie G. If you were the best undercover agent in the world and

your informant wasn't as good as they claimed to be, you couldn't buy drugs off Tweety Bird. So, it was imperative that I stressed the importance of in-depth debriefings of informants and then corroborating the information they provided.

Good informants equaled good cases; bad informants equaled bad cases; it was that straightforward. Throughout my tenure as a special agent with the DEA, safety was always a priority. Safety for me, for my fellow agents, and for the ones I had the honor to lead was always paramount. On more than one occasion I butted heads with agents who were willing to stick their neck out a little bit and sacrifice safety.

Before a DEA unit goes on a drug deal, a briefing is held, and each agent is assigned a particular task during the drug transaction. All the agents rely on the other agents to perform their assigned task. If one link in the chain is broken, then potentially a dangerous situation could arise. The most danger occurs when an undercover agent deviates from his prearranged activities while working undercover. Lesson learned!

Training sessions were a collateral duty. Amidst full-throttle drug investigations, I imparted knowledge from experience to state and local police officers in the Midwest and crossed borders to share the knowledge with Peruvian and Thai police law enforcement officers at all levels. I especially liked the times I spent with my students after the training sessions were over.

First, they loved to have a drink as did most cops during that time. Second, all the training agents also loved to have a drink.

MORE ALCOHOL

Back to the cocktails with local police. During that time my go-to drink was nicknamed the 'See Through.' A more appropriate description would be a four-to-six-ounce glass filled

with vodka and ice with a Twist of lemon. I never traded in my glass and always kept the numerous twists of lemon in the glass as a personal reminder of how many see-throughs I had consumed. The irony of my attempts to manage my alcohol consumption was that it never mattered how many lemon twists remained in the glass.

THE TRAINEES

So, I found it incredibly refreshing to mingle with mostly younger state and local drug agents eager to hear more about my stories and techniques. They also were not shy about cases that they were involved in and were eager to share them. The intensity of their enthusiasm as well as mine, encouraged me to keep on participating in training classes no matter how busy I was. The specific techniques that both I and my training buddies taught saved many drug deals and lives. Every DEA agent involved in the training sessions was highly qualified and experienced.

None of the training guys had to rely on books or notes to teach their trade. They relied strictly on memories of past deals they had personally participated in and learned from. When each trainer was introduced, a little bit about his background was provided to ensure the trainees that what they were getting was the real stuff. When the trainers started talking, the room fell silent, and the eyes of young enthusiastic future drug agents were locked on the agent in the front of the room. Many times, at the end of a presentation the trainees would stand and applaud. It was probably the most gratifying part of my various duties.

THE TRAUMA TEAM

In the transitional 80s, right up until my retirement in 2000, I found myself as a representative of the DEA's trauma team.

Always on call for critical incidents, I was fortunate enough to only have to respond to one incident. The lessons earned during the training sessions to become a trauma team member carry on to this day and have benefited many civilian families who have lost loved ones.

4

Enter Cocaine

Jump into the chaotic era of the late 1970s and 1980s, where the landscape of law enforcement was forever altered by a formidable adversary—cocaine. This wasn't just a problem; it was a national crisis, a challenge that pushed the boundaries of danger for officers on the front lines. The culprit? Cocaine, unleashed upon the United States in staggering quantities by the infamous Colombian drug traffickers, with the Medellin cartel leading the charge.

Miami became a city thrust into the limelight as a major distribution hub for these territorial and ruthless traffickers. The battlegrounds shifted to the streets of Miami and Fort Lauderdale, where constant shootings became the norm. Colombian cocaine trafficking organizations clashed fiercely, turning South Florida into a war zone. The stakes were high, and the danger soared as the traffickers relentlessly hunted down informants and law enforcement personnel embedded within their secretive organizations.

The toll of this drug war was measured in blood. Miami witnessed such a surge in violence that outdoor freezer trailers were brought in to store the mounting corpses. Between 1980

and 1981 alone, the city recorded a staggering 1,000 homicides, a grim testament to the ruthless grip of cocaine on the region. Yet, this number barely scratched the surface, omitting those who met gruesome fates in the Everglades, becoming alligator fodder, or a feast for the sharks in the Gulf of Mexico.

But this wasn't just a Miami problem. The tentacles of the traffickers reached far and wide, forging alliances with dealers across the United States who craved a pure product at enticing prices. Amidst this chaos, unsung heroes emerged within the DEA stationed in the epicenters of Fort Lauderdale and Miami. These fearless agents weren't bystanders; they were warriors engaging in constant battles with the relentless traffickers.

There were also hundreds of agents stationed in cities like Denver, Omaha, Indianapolis, Kansas City, Tulsa, Nashville, Louisville, Baltimore, Milwaukee and Boston who were fighting a similar battle and whose goal was to get to the drug dealers who were supplying their cities. Those agents ended up in source cities like Miami, Fort Lauderdale, the Texas border and Southern California trying to cut the head off the snake before moving on to a new case.

5

The First Years

Long before the Miami deal, I attended basic agents' training school during March of 1972 but won't dwell much on that except to say that training was tough and unforgiving. In about the sixth week of an eight-week course, I suffered an injury which almost caused things to go south. I sprained my ankle while playing basketball with some of my classmates and was told it would take several weeks to heal if the heel was rested.

My foot was x-rayed, and it was determined to be a serious ankle sprain. My class counselor called me to his office and said, "Bill, you have one of two choices: either drop out of the class and recycle to the next class or tape up every morning and hope that you could make it through the class you are currently in." That class included one-mile runs!

Before responding, I rolled the dice and answered, "I'll continue marching and taping up for the morning workouts." Fortunately, I made it through although about 30% of the guys that started didn't for one reason or another. After graduating basic agent training, I was informed that I would be heading to Chicago and working out of the Chicago regional office.

Upon arriving in Chicago, I was assigned to group three and reported way earlier in the day than required. The group was a tight unit of about 10 agents all of whom seemed very close to each other and as the new guy was greeted with a whole lot of skepticism.

My role in the group was clearly defined, which initially involved washing a lot of other agents' official government vehicles. (OGVs) or getting the more senior agents in the group coffee in the morning. I fully expected this based on the briefings I received from my class counselor and was eager to get going with real DEA work.

Six months of watching other agents making buys and doing surveillance, I thought the guys in the group began to realize that they would not be able to dampen my enthusiasm. Because of this, I had the opportunity to make a couple of purchases which involved small quantities of cocaine and heroin.

After one of the buys which occurred in an alley at 26th and Maplewood in Chicago, I returned to the office when a seasoned agent passed me in the hall and commented, "I hear that you bought some dope."

I very proudly responded, "I did, an ounce of heroin."

"Did you get it off a black guy or a Puerto Rican?"

"It was a Puerto Rican, sir."

"The seasoned agent simply said, "Oh."

Shortly thereafter I did make a buy off a black guy on Chicago's West Side. Once again when I returned to the office the same seasoned agent said, "I heard you made another buy and wondered if it was from a black guy or a Puerto Rican."

"It was a black guy."

To this the agent replied, "You are now a real agent!" and shook my hand.

Also, while in Chicago my supervisor assigned me to a senior agent with the objective being to buy an ounce of cocaine. The street name for the cocaine was Peruvian pink. All the necessary arrangements were made for the surveillance, and it was off to the races. Peruvian pink was very rare, and everybody was interested to see how the deal turned out. Kenny, the principal undercover agent, and I then drove to a quiet bar on the near North Side of Chicago while under surveillance of Group 3 agents.

Shortly after entering the bar, a dark skinned, short Latin man entered the bar and approached Ken, who had previously provided our descriptions to Lupe. After greeting each other, we began negotiating with Lupe. Although my role was just to observe and listen, I couldn't help during breaks in conversation to stick in my two cents.

During one of these breaks in conversation I noticed Kenny, who was sitting to my left, had his head slumped down. The bad guy made the same observation, and I thought we both came to the same conclusion that Kenny had died of a heart attack.

Lupe asked, "Is he dead?"

"Ah, don' know."

"I'm outta here," Lupe blurted out.

"Wait! Kenny, Kenny!" I turned to attempt to awaken my partner.

After gathering myself, I shook Kenny a little, and he woke right up. Both the bad guy and I looked at him and wondered what had just happened. Kenny could tell that we didn't understand and simply said, "Forget it."

We continued with the negotiations and ended up buying an ounce of cocaine which turned out to be 97% pure. Although the bad guy didn't want to deal with us anymore, I did find out why Kenny nodded off in the middle of intense negotiations. It turns out, he told me as soon as they got in the car after the transaction, that Kenny had a case of narcolepsy and routinely fell asleep, sometimes in the most unusual circumstances. He asked me not to say anything because that condition would disqualify Kenny from the job.

I never said a word until several years later when I confided in another partner, Herb, who I trusted implicitly, about the incident. Herb said that he was surprised I never mentioned it and probably I was the only agent in the Chicago division that didn't know about Kenny's narcolepsy.

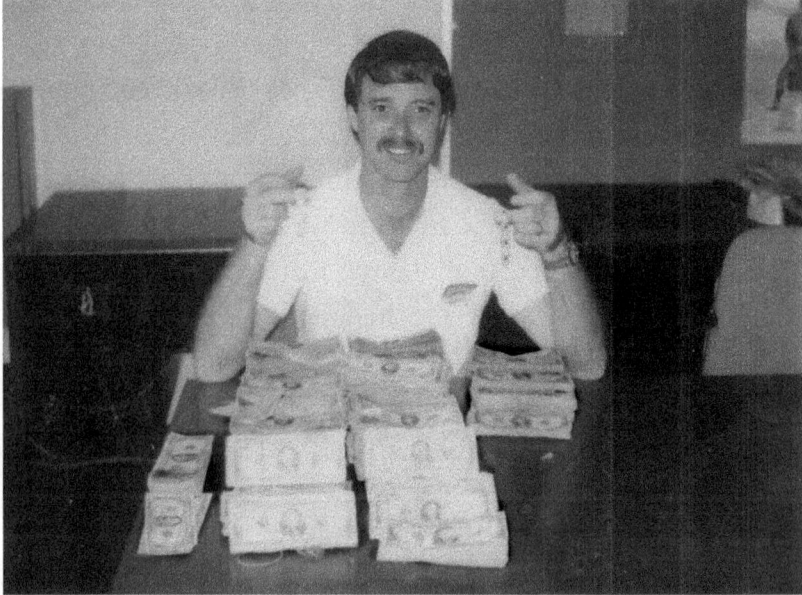

First large money seizure with Group 3 in Chicago

6

Deep Cover

While the above was going on, apparently some behind-the-scenes activities were happening with Chicago Regional management. A lot of drugs were being sold and used on college campuses throughout the country during the early 1970s, and an aggressive president of Southern Illinois University in Carbondale, IL, called the acting regional director of the Chicago office and requested that he send some agents to Carbondale to try to clean up the mess. No attention was paid to those many students who were using drugs nor any attention to students dealing marijuana. Enough hard drugs were being sold to keep the agents busy.

The goal of this and future assignments was to identify and make buys off 'students' who were sources of supply for the real students on campus. The agents assigned quickly learned that there was a hardcore group of drug dealers, enrolled as students, but spending most of their time dealing drugs.

Five other agents along with me were selected for the chore mostly because of our age and looks, long hair and beards. During about March of 1973, the six agents and a supervisor traveled to Southern Illinois University in Carbondale with fake identification and rented apartments.

It didn't take long to get connected to the drug trade and over the next several months the agents bought heroin, LSD, cocaine and barbiturates from 11 Carbondale students and six dealers who were not students. The non-students supplied the campus with drugs, including some of the 11 Carbondale students that we did arrest. When the agents ran out of money allocated for drug purchases, they arrested the group of dealers and sent a strong message to Carbondale.

Five of the Carbondale, Illinois undercover agents

Not long after the Carbondale special assignment, the President of University of Indiana in Bloomington, Indiana, placed a phone call to the same regional director and essentially the same agents were sent to Bloomington, IN, for a couple of months. This repeated itself with both the University of Illinois in Normal, Illinois, and the University of Wisconsin, Madison. Each special assignment lasted two to three months, involved agents living full-time in the various cities and adopting a completely undercover lifestyle.

34

While working these four special assignments, the agents, including me, would frequent local bars and basically get the word out that there was some new money in town that was looking for sources of whatever kind of drug the prospective seller was involved with. It was no hard chore to line up deals with either students on the campus or drug suppliers who were supplying the students with drugs. I was fortunate enough to have been provided with two good informants from the Indianapolis office. They had obviously been trained very well and kept me extremely busy buying every type of drug available.

Several interesting things happened while on these assignments, one of which occurred in Bloomington, Indiana, when I mistakenly set up two drug deals at the same time. When I realized this, I simply called the dealers and decided to meet one of them on one side of the University of Indiana sign and immediately thereafter planned to meet the second dealer on the other side of the sign. Both deals went as smooth as silk.

Another interesting thing happened again while in Bloomington. I met a guy in a local bar who said he could supply unlimited quantities of pharmaceutical drugs. This was right at the beginning of the Bloomington, Indiana, special assignment, and I felt pretty good about both the guy and his source of supply. I set up the deal to occur in the undercover apartment the agents had rented for the next morning. At the appointed time, both guys showed up at our door, one of whom was carrying a big green duffel bag like a military duffel bag.

After introductions, the guy who brought the bag in opened it up and showed me and some other agents a duffel bag full of pharmaceuticals, all contained in the original bottles in which the pharmacies received their drugs. Because of the large amount, the agents couldn't buy all of them nor did they want to arrest

anybody so early in the investigation. So, we basically told the two dealers that we were not interested in their products. "We are looking for harder drugs like cocaine, heroin, LSD, etc."

Working the streets in Bloomington, Indiana

Although it was difficult letting that many drugs walk out our apartment door, the fact that they turned the dealers away cemented our reputations as being drug dealers and certainly not the police. The duffel bag full of drugs and the nonchalant attitude of the two dealers that offered to sell them convinced us that there was a problem on campus.

An interesting thing that occurred was at the time we had to use credit card numbers and go through an operator, believe it or not, to talk to our bosses in Chicago and report our progress. One of the agents made a phone call that was listened to by an operator who had a friend who was a drug dealer. The agent was just reporting about the purchases made the day prior and the

amount of money that was spent to give the boss an idea of how we were doing.

The operator notified her dealer friend who immediately spread the word that DEA agents had come from Carbondale to clean up Bloomington. Because of this, we had to return to home bases for a two-week period before we returned. Most of our physical descriptions were on the street having been provided by the Carbondale defendants.

During that two-week time, I let my facial hair grow and at the encouragement of my two main informants in Bloomington, I bought a brown leather floppy hat and a thigh length brown leather jacket. When I showed up again in Bloomington, the informants indicated that my new look would make it much easier to buy drugs. And they weren't kidding!

My new look precluded a lot of the questions about my legitimacy as a real drug dealer. In fact, the longer the agents in Bloomington and the longer my hair and beard grew, the more people wanted to deal with me. Toward the end of the deployment, my hair was down to my shoulders and my beard down to my Adam's apple. Remember, this was the '70s, The Beatles and Woodstock.

The operation lasted for several months and was significantly more successful than Carbondale. About 50 people were arrested during raids which were conducted in early 1974. Purchased during the Bloomington operation included heroin, cocaine, LSD, MDA and PCP.

The operations conducted at the University of Illinois, Normal, and the University of Wisconsin ended up with basically the same results. The one difference was that the local Madison police department provided us with the name of a person considered to be the largest cocaine dealer in that city.

Prior to establishing a base in Madison, I sent an informant I had from the Milwaukee office to Madison. The informant was given instructions to hang out at certain bars that the cocaine dealer frequented. The informant was also provided with a physical description of the target which obviously included his name and the names and physical descriptions of his associates which had been provided by the Madison Police Department.

After getting established in Madison, it didn't take long for the coke dealer to agree to meeting me. The informant, while working by himself, met the target, Jake, and talked about his friend, that being me, who was looking for a new cocaine source and had plenty of money. I ended up making several drug cocaine buys off the target.

Prior to one of the buys which occurred in Jake's new Cadillac, he brought out an ounce or two of cocaine and laid several lines on the armrest telling me to snort with him. At the same time, a Latin male approached the Cadillac and stood on the passenger side with his right hand in an overcoat pocket pointing either a gun or a finger at me.

Prior to that, the Madison police had told me that I would run into that situation. The Madison police officers found a doctor who might be able to give me some kind of medical excuse not to snort cocaine. Instead of a medical excuse, the doctor gave me a pill which was designed to work in my urinary tract causing my urine to turn red.

Trusting that the pill would work, I told the cocaine dealer that my blood pressure was sky high and if I did any coke, it would kill me. I told the dealer that it was so high I was bleeding and urinating blood. Jake told me that I had to prove that to him, so Jake and I went into the bar adjacent to where the Cadillac was parked, and Jake and the Latin male stood on each side of me as I urinated into the urinal.

As fate would have it, the urine came out red. When Jake and his compadre saw that, they both turned and made a hasty retreat into the bar. Fortunately, they got out before realizing, like I did, that whatever the pill did, caused the urinal to "stain" a light-colored red. After a few flushes the pink stain disappeared, and I could rest easy.

Just prior to rounding up the rest of the Madison dealers, I arranged for a transaction with Jake involving about a half pound of cocaine which was supposed to be a sample for a larger transaction. During that time, a half pound of cocaine was unheard of, especially in a small City like Madison.

When Jake showed up at the location in Madison, he showed me the bag of cocaine, after which I gave an arrest signal to the surveillance agents, and Jake was arrested while sitting in his new Cadillac. When dealers use vehicles to deliver drugs, those vehicles are subject to seizure which is what was done with the Cadillac.

Because of the late hour, I drove Jake's vehicle home waiting to surrender the Cadillac to the U.S. marshals the next morning. Before leaving my residence the next day, I took a dirty blanket that I had seen in the trunk the night before and shook the debris into my yard trying to clean the car up before surrendering it to the marshalls.

I didn't think anything about the Cadillac or the dirty blanket until the next spring when dozens of marijuana plants started growing in my backyard. For some reason it completely escaped me that the debris I was looking at on the blanket was in fact marijuana seeds. They grew right in the same area where I grew my tomatoes, so it was an easy choice to till the ground and plant my tomatoes.

During the Bloomington, Normal and Carbondale, Illinois, and Madison special assignments, I learned several lessons. First, after having worked undercover on about 50 or 60 drug buys, I knew everything drug dealers could throw at us to determine whether we were the police. Being cornered in a smoke-filled apartment with a half a dozen heroin addicts shooting up and asking me to join them tests both me and my training.

I also learned some strategies for dealing with them when they were suspicious of the undercover agent. Lastly and most importantly, I learned that if I had a group of individuals in a community dealing drugs, these dealers could be disrupted with police intervention, the right amount of funds, and highly trained undercover officers who could dance around all the tricks the dealers used.

What the operations accomplished at least for a period was that drug trafficking literally came to a halt in the above cities, and the people who were dealing drugs were taken off the streets. Although at the time, it seemed like the only accomplishment was the local effect of the operations.

Many years later during 1995 in response to the ongoing drug crisis in the United States, The Drug Enforcement Administration created what became known as MET teams (Metropolitan Enforcement Teams) The purpose of these teams was to deploy to drug hotspots located throughout the United States and make cases on sources of supply and dealers in the cities who requested and received DEA assistance.

Often the deployments would occur in areas not normally serviced by the local DEA office. Once deployed, a group of 10 to 12 DEA agents would join with local partners, gather intelligence, identify targets and go after them. Ironically, while assigned to

New Orleans, I had the opportunity to supervise a great group of guys who along with me were assigned to a MET team.

One of the assignments I oversaw within central Louisiana involved a complete block in Alexandria, La that was controlled by the drug dealers. After several weeks of gathering intelligence, making buys, and conducting surveillances, a wiretap was placed on the phone of the main target. I was told no other wiretaps had been conducted up until that point by a MET team. Lucky for me, on a night that I assigned myself to monitor the wiretap, a five-kilogram deal was discussed between the main target in Louisiana and his source of supply in Houston, TX. I contacted an IRS CID agent that I had worked with in the past and coordinated the arrest of the Houston source of supply that resulted in the seizure of five kilograms of cocaine and the arrest of the main source of supply.

Not too long after the five-kilogram seizure, indictments were returned against all the drug dealers who lived on that street in central Louisiana. Prior to the arrests which were conducted at 5a.m., a lieutenant with the local police department started smoking some good old southern briskets. After the arrests went down, all the police officers and agents met at the lieutenant's house, sat back, drank a beer, and enjoyed the best brisket I had ever eaten. The most satisfying result of the above wiretap was that the individuals who lived on the block occupied by the drug dealers were now free to go about their daily business without worrying about drive-by shootings and overdoses.

7

More Undercover

During the spring of 1973, I got word that one of the individuals who was arrested in the southern Illinois raids wanted to work a deal out with the government and give what was known as a proffer. A proffer was an off the record interview that the defendant provides the government to allow it to assess the value of the information provided during the interview.

I met with the potential informant who told me a story I had a hard time believing and left the informant for a few minutes to talk to my supervisor who was a street hardened agent with years of experience. The supervisor had the informant tell the story all over again.

The story was that the informant had access to a guy who could provide millions of hits of mini-bennies and that the same individual had access to people in Mexico who routinely dealt in million hit quantities. (A hit is the equivalent of one dosage unit.) Mini-benny was an amphetamine used by housewives, truck drivers and college students for an energy boost. Mini bennies were commonly referred to as white crosses on the street.

The informant was unable to provide any additional information regarding the organization she belonged to because

she was at such a low level. After grilling her, the supervisor and I both decided to pursue the informant's source of supply. The supervisor told me that the informant sounded legitimate and that we would have the informant place a phone call to the target, Richard Provot, and introduce me over the telephone to set up a deal.

Although we initially talked about dealing in million hit quantities, my supervisor thought, and as it turned out rightfully so, that if I discussed quantities with Richard, we should limit it to a quarter million hits so as not to set off his paranoia. A mistake frequently made by police or federal undercover agents was ordering too much and causing the drug dealer to become paranoid with a large order and without any previous successful transactions.

The informant that was being interviewed placed a recorded telephone call to Richard who lived in a suburb of Chicago, Illinois. The informant told the target that she had an individual that was interested in purchasing a quarter million tablets. The informant told Richard she had done business on many occasions with this guy and further that she trusted him implicitly. After the informant massaged the target with words of confidence, Richard said to put him on the phone so they could negotiate directly.

At that point both the supervisor and I felt that Richard's motivation was strictly greed and a prime motivator. I got on the phone and after a brief introduction, Richard cut right to the chase and asked me how many I wanted. I told him that my preference would be a million tablets but was reluctant to do that big of a deal on the first go-around. This occurred in mid of 1973.

Instead, I told Richard that I would prefer to do 350,000 hits as a sample. Although not a small deal by any token of the

imagination, the 350,000 deal would make both Richard and me comfortable with each other before doing a million. Although of course, neither the government nor I had no intention of parting with $175,000.

With my defenses somewhat lowered, Richard told me that 350,000 hits sounded good and that he would charge me .65 cents per tablet. To look legitimate, I haggled with him about the price. Richard agreed to a discount so the price for the whole lot would be $175,000. He accepted my price without any further negotiations. I was to bring the money, and Richard would bring the drugs to the restaurant meeting spot. I offered one last warning: "There better not be any changes in the plans because if there were, I'm out!"

A meeting time and place was set in a north suburb of Chicago. Richard and I gave each other physical descriptions and set the plan in motion. Because we had a couple days before the transaction, my supervisor got the group of agents together and formulated plans for the surveillance which was to be conducted prior to and during the transaction.

Because of the large amount of drugs involved, the intention from the very beginning was to arrest Richard once I saw the drugs. Although I would have $175,000 stored in the trunk of the Official Government Vehicle, I would only show it to Richard as a last resort. (DEA's vehicle Fleet are just regular cars with no police equipment visible.)

Because I was literally a new agent, the supervisor met the surveillance team without me and told them to be particularly cognizant of everything that was going on during the actual transaction, so nobody got hurt. Surveillance of drug deals or drug dealers had several goals, the first of which was to protect the undercover agent and informant, if one was involved, and

the second goal was to obtain additional evidence against the defendant or the defendants who might be on the scene but not negotiating with the undercover agent. Many times, drug dealers used other individuals to conduct counter surveillance to determine if the police may be conducting surveillance in unmarked vehicles.

Because Richard was so relaxed on the telephone, it was decided that I would bring a flash roll (government funds used to show but not spend) but try to Bogart my way into seeing the drugs without using the flash roll. The supervisor instructed me that if I was not able to see the drugs without money, I was to walk Richard to the OGV, pop open the trunk and give Richard a quick look at the cash, $175,000.

Anything happening at that point might be considered a robbery. Consequently, I was to give a prearranged sign, clearly visible to surveillance agents, indicating problems and requesting backup. Since this was not long after the college special assignments, I still had my brown floppy hat which I would use for an arrest signal by taking it off as Richard approached the OGV.

On the day of the deal, my group had a pre-deal meeting, and some other support agents borrowed from other enforcement groups. All details regarding the deal, what I would be driving, what I would be wearing, where I would go, what I would do, what Richard would be driving, and his physical description were discussed as well as the time and place of the deal. It was made clear to me, just as in basic agent training, that I was not to vary from the game plan that was discussed. It was also decided that the supervisor would have the point (which meant that he would be the agent closest to me).

After the group meeting, we all left the federal building in

Chicago and started heading up to Waukegan to the restaurant/ bar. On the ride up to Waukegan, I was nervous, this being the first large drug transaction I would be involved in as an undercover agent. I was more concerned about my performance in front of my group than anything the bad guy might do. I knew that surveillance would be just as edgy as they feared a mistake made by a new agent. Once I arrived, I pulled into the parking lot of the restaurant and entered the bar.

Finally, entering the bar, I observed a guy who fit the description of the man I had been negotiating with on the phone and approached him. He introduced himself, and Richard acknowledged the introduction. We each had a soft drink during which time they sized each other up. I specifically took every chance I could to see if Richard was armed, and Richard was probably doing the same with me although my .38 Smith & Wesson was tucked in the back of my pants and not exposed in any way.

After Richard felt comfortable, he told me that he had a Volkswagen of a certain color parked in the parking lot and that he would leave the restaurant and enter the Volkswagen. Richard said the car was where the drugs were located. Much to my amazement, I had anticipated a much more rigorous examination by Richard to verify information that the informant had provided. Richard asked me a series of questions verifying information that the informant had provided him based on the instructions provided by me. I was prepared for any examination about my credibility, but it was better to be safe than sorry. Richard then got up and left the restaurant, while I waited about five minutes before exiting.

I never forgot what happened next. As I was pushing the restaurant door open my .38 slipped down the crack in my back

which made it out of reach. Having to think on my feet, I quickly turned around, closed the interior restaurant door, and in the alcove retrieved my weapon, this time placing it in my jeans on the side so I could retrieve it quickly if necessary.

When I walked from the door the second time, all I could think of was surveillance, having seen the gun drop and the grief I would have to put up with whether the deal went or not. I looked around the parking lot and saw the Volkswagen with a large Afghan dog sitting in the front seat. Richard forgot to mention the dog. Of course, at this time I was thinking *Maybe it's attack trained?* I was unable to see any of the several surveillance vehicles in the area which meant that Richard couldn't see them either, and that was a good thing!

I walked to the Volkswagen, opened the door, and saw a suitcase in the back seat. Before I could say anything about the dog, Richard motioned for the dog to get into the back seat. Richard asked me where the money was, and I told him it was in the trunk of a car in the parking lot and that I would retrieve it as soon as I saw that Richard had the drugs. Thankfully the dog remained calm and didn't pose any type of threat.

Richard must have been a little bit nervous making this big of a deal with a new guy because that was the second time he asked me where the money was, the first time being in the bar.

Again, to my amazement, Richard said the drugs were in a suitcase in the back seat of the Volkswagen right next to the dog. Richard invited me to pop open the suitcase and verify that it contained the mini bennies.

With a bit of difficulty, I turned around and reached over the front seat then opened the suitcase which contained several packages wrapped in a way that was very consistent with the way shipments of mini bennies were transported, 25,000 hits of

speed per package for a total of 350,000 tablets. At this time, I told Richard that I would go get the money and sit tight. I exited the car and started walking away while at the same time giving the pre-arranged arrest signal which had been discussed prior to the deal.

Within seconds, the parking lot filled with the surveillance agents who effected the arrest of Richard without incident. The drugs were seized by surveillance agents who had been watching the negotiations from both inside the bar and in the parking lot. The drugs were transported back to the Chicago office where they were processed and prepared for delivery to the Chicago laboratory.

With a smile on my face, I took a deep breath for the first time since I got into the Volkswagen. The surveillance agents who transported the drugs to the Chicago office then transferred them to me who processed them and with one of the surveillance agents delivered the drugs to the Chicago lab. At the time I was told by a chemist in the Chicago lab that this seizure was the biggest Mini Bennie seizure that the chemist could remember in the Chicago division.

8

Climbing the Ladder

Within a day or two, I got a call that Richard was interested in providing a proffer and was willing to work with DEA to make a case against his source of supply. He was interested in giving DEA the intelligence he had regarding the drug trafficking organization he belonged to. As it turned out, Richard's knowledge was extensive and involved people not only on the West Coast but also in Mexico.

I met Richard at his residence and was told that an accomplice of his, Steve Issod, was in possession of 750,000 tablets of mini bennies. After a significant amount of debriefing which included much more detailed information about the organization Richard worked with including names and locations, I was getting itchy to make a move on the organization.

Shortly after our meeting, I decided to have Richard place a call to this guy, Steve Issod, to introduce me on the phone and get Steve to deliver the 750,000 tablets to me. As a rookie, this even seemed too easy, but I figured that if I didn't try, nothing would ever happen. Richard placed the phone call to Steve and after initial conversations about me and an appropriate background story, Steve agreed to talk to me on the phone.

Richard provided the cover story that I had created. When Steve and I talked, Steve asked me no brainer questions about my connection with Richard.

"So, Richard told me you guys have done business before?"

"Yeah, we did. Heard the same about you and Richard (no response) anyhow how do you want to do this?"

"I'll need cash, no bullshit."

"I've got the cash, and Richard will vouch for it."

"Just as long as you know."

"Where did you first meet him?

"That city north of Milwaukee with the university."

"Oh, that's where Cathy's from." (Cathy was the girl from Carbondale who introduced me to Richard.)

"Yeah, she did some work for me up there, in fact she drove some stuff to me from Richard."

"He told me about that."

"Yeah, but . . ."

"Give me a day, I'll be in touch."

All the information discussed during the above conversation had previously been provided to both Cathy and Richard in debriefings. Based on the questions that Steve asked it was clear Steve had done his homework and was attempting to get me in a trap. The conversation that I had with Steve was basic stuff and easily handled. The way I delivered my answers was almost as important as the content of the answers.

During this and subsequent telephone conversations I had with Steve, we planned to meet at O'Hare Airport on June 8, 1973. Steve said that he would fly in from San Diego to Chicago and that he would meet me in a terminal at O'Hare at which time he would provide me with the baggage claim tickets for the

luggage containing the pep pills. Other than passing the baggage claim tickets no other acknowledgment between us was to occur.

After I claimed the baggage, I would rejoin Steve, and we would proceed to retrieve the money. Of course, during this time there was no airport security so there were no problems moving freely about the airport. After that conversation, I met with my supervisor and explained what was hopefully going to occur. My supervisor was convinced this was a good deal. I gathered the group of agents I was assigned to and formulated plans for the arrest of Steve after I took possession of the suitcases.

On June 7, 1974, Steve contacted me and told me what flight he would be on and at what terminal and gate number I should meet him. We also exchanged physical descriptions of each other including what color shirts and pants we would be wearing. During the morning of June 8, my group conducted an additional briefing making sure that everybody knew what their assignments were and who would be the point men making sure I was covered.

After the meeting, the surveillance team and I drove out to O'Hare Airport to initiate the plan. I went to the pre-arranged terminal and gate and waited for the arrival of Steve at O'Hare. Not long after the team was set up and in position and I was at the designated meeting spot, I saw a guy matching Steve's description walking down the terminal in my direction. As we had previously decided, Steve would quickly hand off the baggage tickets to me and after I retrieved the bags, I would meet Steve in the lower part of O'Hare and go to my car to retrieve the money.

As planned, when we passed each other, Steve handed me two baggage claim tickets and just kept on walking, not even acknowledging or looking at me. I walked down to the baggage claim area, and after what seemed like a long time, the bags

arrived, and I grabbed them. The surveillance team knew that Steve was in a different part of the airport and were maintaining surveillance on him. My supervisor approached me, and we opened the bags in a restroom observing many packages that were wrapped consistent with bulk quantities of white crosses.

After confirming the two suitcases were full of drugs, a surveillance agent radioed that the arrest could be made. Steve was in cuffs within seconds of the radio transmission. The arrest was uneventful. Any attempts to question Issod were met with the word "lawyer" so they had to quit the questioning and lock him up. This shipment ended up being 1,000,000 tablets of which 700,000 tablets contained illegal amphetamine, and 300,000 tablets contained caffeine. (I still couldn't figure out why Steve delivered a million tablets instead of the 750,000 ordered.) That was a drug dealer's way of being greedy and ripping off his buyer. It happened all the time especially with powdered controlled substances when the dealer added what was known as an adulterant, which is an inert substance used only to add weight to the product as in many cases with cocaine and heroin.

It seemed as though Steve and related crime partners were much bigger than anticipated. I later discovered that between May 31,1973 and July 20 of 1974, they delivered almost two kilos of cocaine to Steve and Richard and another individual and almost three million tablets of mini bennies to the same individuals. The above was significant because the government wasn't involved in any of those deliveries and all of them were conducted under the radar.

There exists a law in Title 21 of the United States code, section 846, which is the conspiracy law. The law states that if two or more individuals agree to commit a specific crime and have the intent to carry out the crime and commit an overt act

in furtherance of a crime, they would be guilty of conspiracy. Of course, the government must prove beyond a reasonable doubt these elements: agreement, intent, and committing an overt act in furtherance of the crime.

9

Transfer To Milwaukee

Following the completion of the above case, I resumed the duties I had been performing prior to the arrest of Steve. One of the duties which was noteworthy or not so much was when the Chicago office had a shortage of government vehicles for agents to use both to and from work. The reason that the government-provided vehicles on a 24-hour basis was because agents were on call 24 hours a day and needed to be able to respond in a quick manner from their homes or wherever they might be. I was assigned a senior agent as my partner who happened to live in Crown Point, Indiana.

That was fine except that I lived in Wauconda, Illinois, and because of the shortage of vehicles, I had to pick my partner up in Crown Point every morning and deliver us to the Chicago office for work. When we got done with work, which was never earlier than seven p.m. and usually much later, I would drive to Crown Point, drop him off, drive to Wauconda, go to sleep and repeat the trip twice a day, every day for about a month. Although my senior partner was a great guy, I began to tire of the long periods of time we had spent in the car on the way to work in traffic. The total time that I spent on the road during this month was approximately four to five hours a day. It would have been significantly longer; however, the travel times began very early in the morning and ended very late at night, no rush hour. Because of the length of the commute, I heard about an opening in the Milwaukee office and called an agent that I knew to inquire about the driving time to the Milwaukee office from any of the nearby suburbs. I was told about a half hour commute. Because of its short drive, I applied to the Milwaukee office.

During 1974, I transferred to Milwaukee, Wisconsin, at the encouragement of an agent who was stationed in Milwaukee. Augie was an incredible undercover agent. After transferring there, I met a Wisconsin State Department of Justice Agent, Mike. During the initial meeting, Mike and I found that we both attended the same college, University of Illinois, Chicago Circle campus and in fact recognized each other.

First car I seized

Mike told me that he had recently arrested an individual who, when debriefed, identified a large group of individuals operating in North Central Wisconsin, Chicago, San Diego and

Mexico who were distributing very large quantities of white crosses/mini bennies. It didn't take a rocket scientist to figure out that his informant was talking about the very same group of people that I had been involved with while working in Chicago.

The odds of the above coincidences were incredible and hard to believe at first until Mike gave me an opportunity to interview his informant. The informant verified all the information I had gathered in Chicago after the arrests of Richard and Steve. The informant began providing names of key players in both Wisconsin and California. One of the key players that the informant was still in touch with was a guy by the name of Tim Callen who had the ability to deal directly to the Mexican sources of supply in California, the same sources of supply for the mini bennies that were used by Steve and Rich. Mike and I began to formulate a game plan whereby the informant would introduce me to Tim as a guy with big money who was interested in buying large quantities of mini bennies. I had to scratch my head and wonder what the chances of busting Steve and Richard while assigned to Chicago and then get transferred to Milwaukee and jump on the same case with the same sources of supply.

Plenty of discussion occurred between Supervisors relating to this case about whether I should be used as the undercover agent because my description was clearly well known, by both Steve and Richard. I argued that all I had to do was shave my long scraggly beard, cut my hair a little bit and forget the floppy hat and I would be fine. In the end my argument won and I could continue working undercover. My Milwaukee boss warned me on more than one occasion, "If you get killed, I'll lose my pension." I thought he was just kidding, maybe?

After debriefing the informant, both Mike and I believed that the informant would be more productive being directed by

me because of my knowledge of the organization all the way from Mexico to Wisconsin. Mike and I began a series of phone calls between the informant and Tim during which time the informant told Tim about a friend of his who had a lot of money and was looking for a new source of supply for speed.

Many more details were provided during these conversations about my relationship with the informant, including the fact that I went to high school with him. That was an ouch because as soon as Tim heard about our high school days, he said he'd be happy to do business with me if he saw a high school yearbook with my picture and name in it. At that time, I was working undercover as Bill Bennett.

The informant and I tried but couldn't get Tim off from insisting on seeing my picture in the high school yearbook. It was a lesson learned for a young undercover guy. An agreement was made to plan for a meeting with Tim in San Diego. The informant and I along with a female undercover agent from the west coast would travel to San Diego and meet Tim.

During late June of 1974 the informant and I flew to San Diego and made telephone contact with Tim who at that time was in San Diego. After the telephone negotiations with Tim, I decided it would be best for the informant to set up a solo meeting with Tim. The meeting occurred under the surveillance of agents from the local office, and after the meeting, the informant reported to me that Tim requested a meeting with me at a hotel close to the ocean in San Diego.

I contacted my local DEA support agent and advised him that a meeting was set between me and Tim at the hotel. Arrangements were made for surveillance to be conducted at the hotel during the meeting for my protection. I also decided that it was time during this meeting that a female agent from

the local DEA office would accompany me which always added a little validity to an undercover agent story because there were so few female undercover agents at that time. (Each time I say" I decided" really means with the approval of a supervisor)

Surveillance got set up both inside and outside of the hotel restaurant and on me, Angel, the female undercover agent, and the informant. The informant, along with Angel and me, drove to the hotel and entered it. The informant immediately pointed out Tim. After entering the hotel, we walked to the table where Tim was sitting, and introductions were made. Almost as soon as the introductions were made, Tim asked if I had brought my high school yearbook. Having been prepared for this question I slapped my head and stated, "Boy, am I am asshole!"

I told Tim that when I was packing, I put the yearbook on a coffee table right next to the suitcase so I wouldn't forget it, and when the informant showed up early to pick me up for the airport, I got a little flustered and completely forgot to grab the yearbook. I apologized profusely and stated that I hoped I didn't waste either Tim's time or my time. Tim told me that without the yearbook picture there would be no deal.

Having been taught by many seasoned agents, especially Augie from the Milwaukee office, "When you're wrong be strong," I pointed my finger at Tim and said, "Sorry I forgot the fucking yearbook, but if you're dumb enough to even talk to me and not trust him (pointing at the informant), maybe I'd better hop on the first thing heading east." Tim and I went back and forth, and the deeper Tim dug in his heels, the more aggressive I got. Finally, after reaching an impasse, I said to Tim, "This is really getting old. You figure out what the real problem is. I'll be in town for a day or two, then I'm outta here."

I signaled the female undercover agent and the informant with a wave of the hand and said, "Let's get out of here!"

At that point Tim spoke up. "Hold on! Let's talk this through." This really was him indicating that ultimately the yearbook picture was not a critical issue. Tim then began asking me detailed questions about my relationship with the informant, things we had done together, things that the informant liked to do, how many deals we had done with each other and the quantities of drugs, etc.

Fortunately, from my training and job experience I had answers to those questions without skipping a beat and purposely began acting very agitated. I had plenty of prep time on the flight to San Diego so although the questions were very pointed, they weren't difficult. My agitation with the paranoia of Tim was starting to percolate to the top and Tim could certainly feel it and hear it in the tone of my voice. Angel was also getting agitated and nudged me a couple times before she finally said, "Let's get out of here."

Addressing Tim, I said, "If you have a problem with me, then you must have had a big problem with (the informant). In that case, I don't see the point of proceeding." At that point Tim completely backed off and told me he would contact his sources of supply in Mexico and see what they had to say. Although I didn't know this to be a fact, I strongly suspected that when Tim called up his Mexican sources of supply, he told them that he had seen the yearbook picture because again greed was fogging his decision-making process.

Somewhere between June 25 and June 29, 1974, I was contacted by Tim who advised that his sources of supply wanted to meet me before they conducted any transactions. After the above conversation, I contacted my San Diego contact agent

and determined that I should set up a meeting with the sources of supply that evening at the same restaurant where we had previously met.

Because this was essentially a do-over from the previous meeting, the surveillance meeting was conducted in my motel and plans formulated for the informant and me and Angel to meet the Mexican sources of supply along with Tim at a specific time. After I was advised that surveillance was set up, the informant, Angel, and I proceeded to the hotel restaurant and were greeted by Tim who acted like he had known Angel and me forever. Of course, the informant had previously met the Mexican sources of supply and conducted transactions with them.

After sitting down with Tim, Angel and I couldn't help noticing two Mexican males sitting close to the table we were now occupying. After Tim and I conducted a little bit of small talk, I asked Tim, "Why aren't the Mexicans joining us?"

Tim started providing a lame excuse, "Oh, they're just paranoid." But while he was explaining, I interrupted him and waved the Mexicans over to join the assembled group.

With little hesitation the Mexicans got up and joined us. Using a common strategy utilized by Mexican drug traffickers, Juan and Henry pretended not to be able to understand English. Knowing that without a doubt Juan and Henry could understand English perfectly well, the informant and I began an impromptu discussion about prior drug transactions that had occurred between us. These fictitious drug transactions were solely meant to lend credibility to me as a drug dealer.

We shot from the hip when the informant and I, who were now feeling very comfortable in this type of situation, fabricated several deals that we had allegedly done in the past to add to our credibility with Henry and Juan. Tim even

jumped in and said that although he didn't participate in the deals we were talking about, he was aware of them from talking to the informant.

After it seemed that the tension had left the air and the Mexicans' paranoia had lessened, I ordered a million minnie bennies directly from the Mexican sources of supply, specifically the older one, Henry, who seemed to be the boss. Even though Henry and Juan still pretended that they didn't speak English, they had no problem understanding drug lingo. I knew that going into the meeting. They indicated, through Tim, that they would see what they could do and get back in touch with me to make the final arrangements for the transaction, including a price for the million hits.

I attempted to get them to deliver their product to Chicago, but they indicated, and logically so, that because this was the first transaction, I would have to come to Tim with the money and make my own transportation arrangements. Tim and I agreed to the above arrangements and recommended we stay in touch with each other to complete the transaction. When everybody parted ways, it seemed to Angel and me that the Mexicans were on board and willing to go ahead with the deal. The meeting broke up and we all went our separate ways pending the completion of the transaction.

10

CENTAC 4
(CENTRAL TACTICAL PROGRAM)

In the middle of the above activities, I was summoned to the DEA headquarters in D.C. for what turned out to be a large meeting of DEA agents from throughout the country whose respective cities had been inundated with mini bennies. Headquarters had a program designed to address drug problems that were emerging in different parts of the country, so they formed what was called CENTAC, and this project was going to be known as CENTAC 4. After being designated a CENTAC, all investigative, enforcement and prosecutions would be coordinated to cut the head off the snake.

Agents assigned to the individual cases would report their efforts directly to headquarters, bypassing their local supervisors, which in many cases didn't sit well with the first line bosses. What I learned during these meetings was that mini bennies had become a problem in all parts of the United States, and they were being abused by millions of people.

Additionally, what was very interesting was that when each clandestine lab's pill press struck an individual tablet, a unique mark would be left on the tablet to that press, similar

to a fingerprint. The DEA laboratory in D.C. determined that there were several clandestine pill presses working in Mexico, and in conjunction with the Mexican government discovered the locations of several of them. Sometime either during or shortly after this meeting, a decision was made to have a nationwide roundup of individuals implicated in the cases on or about September 11, 1974.

I continued negotiating for the delivery of a million tablets with Tim; however, little progress was being made, and it was my belief that the two Mexican sources of supply may have figured out that the guy they met in San Diego may have been the same guy who arrested Steve Issod and Richard in the Chicago area. When negotiations with the Mexican sources of supply seemed fruitless, a decision was made to arrest Tim and to turn him into an informant and help set up the two Mexicans.

On July 20, 1974, I planned, after receiving the okay from headquarters, to order a quantity of cocaine from Tim and have it delivered to Chicago. Similar surveillance precautions were made, and I met Tim in a hotel room in Chicago after ordering multiple ounces of cocaine. When the day came, surveillance was established in the hotel and outside the hotel again for security purposes. I checked into a room in the hotel.

After preparations were made, I called Tim and told him I was ready, had the money, and for him to proceed to my hotel room. Shortly thereafter, Tim knocked on the hotel room door and entered. Both he and I were on edge; Tim was worried about getting arrested, and I was worried about getting ripped off. I then attempted to engage in general conversation with Tim to lower his radar which seemed to work. I asked him if he had the stuff to which Tim replied that he did, and he asked me if I had the money to which I replied that I did.

Something unusual occurred next. Tim stepped toward me which immediately caused some concern. He then extended his hand and asked me to shake it and swear that I wasn't a narc. I didn't have any problem with his request, of course, so I shook his hand and said, "Tim, I'm not a narc."

After the handshake, Tim, with a sigh of relief replied, "Good!" and produced the drugs.

After I examined the drugs, I pulled my weapon and told Tim he was under arrest. I then notified the surveillance agents via a DEA radio I had hidden in the hotel room. I requested that they should come to my room and assist me with the defendant, which happened within seconds because they were right next door.

Tim was still scratching his head wondering what the heck had just happened even after the cuffs were put on his wrist. He was in shock. Even before we left the room, Tim uttered, "Lawyer" and that quickly ended all attempts to make him into an informant. Consequently, once again my only option was to lock him up just like we did with Steve.

After the above arrest, little was left for me to do in an undercover capacity. Plenty was left which included gathering telephone records, hotel records, and airplane records. Unfortunately, the Mexicans and other accomplices chose to stay at a hotel near General Billy Mitchell field in Milwaukee and of course during 1974 the hotel only kept hard copies of hotel receipts which were stored in an attic of the hotel in large cardboard boxes and in no order.

I enlisted as much help as I could get to go through the records to find the specific ones relating to the Mexicans and others. Fortunately, friends and I came up with everything we were looking for after a lot of sweating. The hotel, airplane and

telephone records verified witness testimony placing various drug dealers in hotels, on airplanes and making telephone calls during specific times surrounding deals which occurred prior to law enforcement's involvement. (If in 1976 Witness One said that Juan flew to Milwaukee and stayed at such and such hotel, and if I found the record supporting the flight and the hotel stay, that would corroborate the witness's testimony. In addition, the telephone toll records would reflect calls from San Diego to Wisconsin before and after a defendant was in San Diego and Wisconsin.)

Finally, the day arrived for the roundup. When approaching a roundup of that magnitude, coordination is essential between the local DEA offices and their state and local counterparts for the raids to be conducted in a tight time frame. The reason for this is that many of the defendants in these different cities knew each other and if one group was arrested in Chicago, they or their attorneys would certainly notify other defendants who hadn't been arrested and who likely would flee. Although I had just a piece of the overall picture, it was still nerve-wracking making sure that everything was done properly and timely at my end.

Telephone calls were coming in to me from the various arrest teams involved in the arrests and seizures. At the same time, I notified my headquarters' liaison of the progress being made in Wisconsin. Arrests of approximately 100 individuals occurred in the cities of New York, Los Angeles, Portland, Los Angeles, San Francisco, Boston, Seattle, Tucson, Phoenix, Charleston (WV), Green Bay, North Central Wisconsin, Chicago, Denver and some smaller cities. Additionally, 25 other individuals were arrested in Mexico, and four of the clandestine pill presses were seized and destroyed by the Mexican government.

Within days of the above arrests, the administrator of The Drug Enforcement Administration stated that a group of interlocking conspiracies flooded the black market with 3 billion illicit amphetamines known as mini bennies. The value of those tablets each year was about 1.6 billion dollars.

Drugs worth more than one million dollars were seized in connection with the arrests based on the indictments in Milwaukee. Additionally, the Resident Agent in Charge of the Milwaukee DEA office gave a news conference with the Attorney General of the State of Wisconsin and stated that 1.5 million mini bennies, 5 1/2 pounds of cocaine, 12 ounces of heroin and 50 pounds of marijuana were seized because of the Milwaukee indictments. The overall goal of the CENTAC 4 operation was to dismantle the organization responsible for distributing hundreds of millions of minnie bennie tablets throughout the United States. Since the CENTAC 4 operation, mini bennies virtually disappeared from the streets of America.

Looking back, this was a great start to a new career but at the time because I had no experience, it didn't seem like that big of a thing. I believed that this type of case would be like the rest of the ones I would be working on throughout my career, both in scope and results. Little did I know that this case was a cakewalk compared to what was coming down the road.

It did provide me with a template for future cases and how to develop them. It began by making a small buy in Carbondale off a girl who knew a guy in the Chicago area to get transferred to Milwaukee and meeting the guy I went to college with who let me work with a very good informant. Good informants and a lot of luck made a great case. Two and a half years down and plenty to go.

All but one of the defendants in the Milwaukee case were eventually found guilty because of guilty pleas or trials. Most received prison sentences and a strong message had been sent, although apparently as time showed, it wasn't heard.

11
Side Story

Somewhere in the middle of all the above activities and after Steve Issod had been arrested, he did what they called at the time 'fugitated' or when referring to him simply said "He's in the wind," both of which meant that he became a federal fugitive. After things settled down a bit sometime during the late fall or early spring of 1975, I was bored one afternoon. Around 4 p.m. I decided to try to look for and find Steve Issod. The first thing I did was to review Issod's telephone billing statements and frequently called numbers.

After about a half an hour of just calling various numbers from Steve Issod's billing statement and asking to speak to Steve, I finally got a number in Philadelphia, and when I asked for Steve, the person on the other end of the phone said, "Yeah that's me." I immediately recognized the voice as being that of Steve Issod but certainly didn't expect to get that lucky so quickly. On the spur of the moment, I had to do a little improvising. I said that the person who answered the call didn't sound like the guy I was looking for and then asked if he was from Altoona, Pennsylvania.

Steve said that he wasn't, and I apologized for calling the wrong number and hung up. I then planned with the Philadelphia

DEA office to go to the house and arrest Issod. I provided them with a copy of the federal warrant and a physical description of Issod just in case there were any questions. DEA Philadelphia must not have had anything to do that night because later that evening they did arrest Issod. Guess you can run but you can't hide!

12
Tip Of The Spear

As mentioned above, sometime during the 1970s or early 1980s, Colombian drug traffickers began exporting cocaine and marijuana from south Florida. My first involvement with this new trend was when the Milwaukee DEA office received a phone call from the Fort Lauderdale DEA office during late summer 1975. The Fort Lauderdale office forwarded information to us that a trafficker in southern Wisconsin had just received a large shipment of marijuana and was preparing it for distribution.

After the Milwaukee office analyzed the information provided by Fort Lauderdale and verified it through human and telephone toll information, we decided to establish surveillance on a rural farmhouse in Salem, Wisconsin. Because of the location of the farmhouse, it was difficult to maintain a constant eye on the driveway leading to the farmhouse. Charlie, my partner, and I decided to park our car and approach the farmhouse on foot to see if we could get an eye that would reveal important information relating to the load of marijuana.

An abandoned pickup truck was left in a field located adjacent to the farm. Because it was dark out, I didn't have any problem

getting to the pickup and ended up crawling underneath it where Charlie and I could more easily observe a van parked in the farm driveway. We remained there for approximately an hour when some individuals left the farm and began loading the van. During this process, one of the guys walked over to the pickup truck and relieved himself on the tire. It was a pretty close call, and it required very light breathing.

Charlie and I had a DEA portable radio and after the van was loaded, several people re-entered the farmhouse while two guys got into the van and drove down the driveway.

Charlie notified the remaining surveillance agents that it looked like the van had been loaded with marijuana and was leaving the driveway. The two partners maintained surveillance on the farm until they determined that the van had been stopped a couple miles away by their surveillance agents and a large amount of marijuana had been discovered inside the van along with a .357 Magnum and a .38 Smith & Wesson revolver. One of the agents on the surveillance team initiated the process of getting a search warrant for the farm.

It didn't take too long to obtain the search warrant, at which time the surveillance team, Charlie, and I approached the farm and announced that we were federal agents with a search warrant and to open the door. Because guns had been found in the van during the traffic stop, we were very cautious, and when lights went on in the house, we kicked the door in.

There were four occupants in the house who were all placed under arrest, and when the search of the house was conducted, about 600 pounds of marijuana was found. Previously the marijuana seized in the van weighed about 400 lbs. At the time, this was the biggest seizure of marijuana in the state of Wisconsin's history.

All six of the individuals arrested were ultimately convicted in court and sentenced to various amounts of time in jail. What wasn't realized at that moment was that this would be the first of many marijuana and cocaine cases that were made in Wisconsin with drugs originating in Columbia and flowing through Florida. This pattern would repeat itself in every city in the United States no matter what size.

Tip of the Spear marijuana seizure

13

New Sheriff In Town

Sometime in the mid-1970s, Harry, a tall, thin, geeky-looking guy, appeared at the DEA office in Milwaukee seeking to speak with an agent. Fortuitously, I was chosen to talk to him. Before granting him entry, I inquired about his purpose. He promptly flashed credentials from the IRS Criminal Intelligence Division (CID). Unlike the conventional image of IRS employees, CID agents carried guns and delved into investigations involving substantial sums of money, often linked to criminal activities.

Having no knowledge or experience with IRS CID, I quickly learned that I could not tell a book by its cover. In fact, my first thought was that I was being audited but wasn't too worried because at that time I was only making around $14,000 a year. This guy did everything while he was ultimately assigned to DEA. This included one occasion where I was working an undercover case at a nearby airport hotel. During negotiations, it became clear that I needed another undercover agent. I pretended that we had a large quantity of marijuana that was for sale in what turned out to be my first reverse undercover case.

I told the crook to stand by and that I was going to go get my drug guy who just happened to be seated at the same bar where

the crook and I were seated. Originally cast as a surveillance agent but quickly pivoting to that as part of the undercover operation, I gave Harry a quick look at where negotiations were going. He readily accepted the undercover assignment which ended in the arrest of two or three bad guys and the seizure of $100,000 in cash.

The IRS CID agents carried guns and conducted investigations involving large sums of money and tax evasion, typically tied to criminal activities. CID agents were involved in nearly every type of criminal investigation, handling cases like DEA or FBI agents executing search warrants and making arrests This guy proposed a collaboration, suggesting we intertwine money-related cases with drug investigations. His frequent appearances at the DEA office led the office to provide him not only a desk but also space for another CID agent and an IRS intelligence agent.

This partnership spanned two decades, evolving into a remarkable learning experience for both Harry and me. Together we initiated numerous successful cases, forming friendships and traversing the United States to interview witnesses and gather physical evidence. Several years later, another IRS CID agent began working side by side with DEA. What I learned was that Neil Saari was just as tenacious and skilled as Harry was.

14

Keep On Moving

Between CENTAC-4 and CENTAC 20, which occurred in the late 70's, I didn't let a lot of grass grow under my feet. I participated in numerous undercover transactions, some of which, as I looked back at it, had chilling side stories. One occurred when a senior agent in the Milwaukee office told me I could work with one of his informants to make a buy off of two brothers, both of whom were well known to law enforcement. The record checks indicated that during previous contacts with law enforcement, the brothers carried guns which was not unusual but did raise a flag.

As per the routine before making a purchase using an informant, I went to the informant's house escorted by surveillance agents and knocked on his door, expecting him to come out so I could search him in my car. When he didn't come out, I hollered his first name a couple of times before the door opened. When I walked in, the informant looked like he was messed up on something. I was still wearing my floppy leather hat, brown leather jacket, long hippie hair and a big beard.

I asked him what the heck was going on, and he said not to worry about it; he was tripping on LSD. Now, if I had more experience, I would have immediately walked out of the house

and informed the senior agent that the informant could not be used. But I was a rookie, hungry, and wanted to make the buy. The informant and I left, went to a payphone and called the two bad guys to set up a meeting in Milwaukee's near North Side.

I then drove the informant to the meeting spot and saw a white van matching the description given by the two crooks. I parked about a block away and walked to the van. We entered through the side door, and finding no back seats, just took a seat on the floor. Introductions were made, and the crooks' first question was if I had the money. I indicated that I left the money in my car until I could determine if they had the cocaine. They claimed they had the coke and showed it to me after which I directed them to take me to my car to retrieve the money—around $1390 for 1 ounce (about 28 gr) of cocaine.

En route to the car, I started getting questions about whether I was a narc, and if I was, there would be a high price to pay for both the informant and me. During this questioning, I was shocked when the informant opened his big mouth and told the two crooks that I was a DEA agent. The two crooks got tight jaws and pulled over to the side of the road where they intensified their grilling. They were now at a point where things could go south fast and with little notice, so I had to get my head together quickly.

Fortunately, my training kicked in, and I spoke up. "This dumb son of a bitch is high on LSD and doesn't know what the hell he's talking about!" The stronger position I took in not being a narc, the more the brothers backed off, ultimately leading to a successful deal. By now the two bad guys, the informant, and I were in my undercover car.

After some discussion, both brothers agreed that the informant was a scumbag that used too many hallucinogens and

that anything that came out of his mouth was usually garbage. After things settled down in the car, I handed my undercover telephone number to one of the brothers and told them in the future if they wanted to do business, they could contact me directly. One ounce for $1390, and the deal was done. I was far from done with the informant.

When we finished the deal, I had a long talk with the informant about being stupid. In his state of mind, he still didn't get what I was upset about. I never used him again. After the purchase, I returned to the office and processed the cocaine. After processing the dope, I sat at my desk, leaned back and wondered if there was a less stressful occupation that I could be paid for and have as much fun as being a DEA agent. After a short deliberation, I decided against an occupational change.

About one week later, I was contacted by Tim, one of the guys who had sold me the cocaine. He asked if I was still interested in purchasing cocaine from him, and I told him I would be, if the informant wasn't involved. I made plans to pick up the dealer. While I was being surveilled by agents for the Milwaukee office, the dealer directed me to an address on Milwaukee's North Side. He told me where to park and then walked to the door of an apartment.

The door opened after he knocked, and I observed a short heavy-set woman greet him at the door and hand him what turned out to be an ounce of cocaine. The dealer returned to my car and passed the cocaine. After observing it and smelling the ether odor, I handed him $1,500. The dealer returned to the apartment, knocked on the door, and handed the woman the money for the drugs. I could clearly see her as she accepted the drug money.

After we completed the second transaction and identified the woman in the doorway, Nina, we determined that she had a prior conviction for drugs and was connected to some pretty good drug dealers. We essentially repeated the first deal all over again.

Because I had determined that Nina was connected to some higher-level dealers, I got arrest warrants for both her and the guy who handed me the cocaine. After their arrest, both attempted to cooperate, however neither one of them was willing to testify. We got good intelligence from both, but it was basically just raw intelligence that we couldn't act on.

At the time of the above arrest, the relatively new conspiracy laws were being tested throughout the United States, and her attorney, who was a very bright young and aggressive guy, challenged the conspiracy charge that was used against her and the guy I was buying directly from. She eventually went to trial and was convicted. Her accomplice, the one who handed me the cocaine, testified against her! Because both had prior drug convictions, they were both sentenced to prison which almost ended law enforcement's interest in these two-time losers. The other brother was never charged because we didn't want to have the informant anywhere near a witness stand for fear of what he may say or do.

15

You Can't Make This Stuff Up

Another deal happened around the same time when I was introduced to two guys by another informant who claimed they could provide large quantities–many kilos– of cocaine. After the introductions, we identified the crooks and conducted a record check at the Milwaukee Police Department MPD for any prior criminal involvement.

The records check which was conducted through narcotics came back indicating that the two guys had conducted a drive-by shooting at a beauty salon right in the middle of downtown Milwaukee just a week earlier. No other information was provided during the records check. What made it more intriguing was that, according to MPD informants, the beauty salon was financially backed by one of the top organized crime leaders in Milwaukee.

Despite the beauty shop revelation, we debated whether to go ahead with the deal. Based on my gut feeling and a very good informant, we decided to continue negotiations. A meeting was set up with the two crooks for late one evening without the informant. Under close surveillance by the DEA office, I met the crooks, and they began discussing prices and quantities.

☆ ☆

Due to the busy street, we parked on, the crook suggested moving to a dead-end street about a block and a half away. What I didn't realize at the time was that part of the reason the street was busy was because of a co-mingling of the surveillance that was on me, and the Milwaukee Police Department Detective Bureau who was following the two crooks because of the beauty shop shooting. How the two surveillances didn't see each other was a one in a million shot.

Confident in my surveillance, I agreed to the change of location. As they parked the car, they broke out a joint and invited me to join them. I concocted a quick story about why I couldn't smoke, and we continued negotiations. Suddenly, all hell broke loose a few minutes after arriving at the dead-end street. Half a dozen Milwaukee squads and a paddy wagon converged on the two bad guys and me, lights blazing and guns drawn.

Ordered to exit the car with our hands in the air, we were immediately grabbed by a mix of plainclothes and uniformed officers. I didn't have any identification, but did have my trusty Smith & Wesson .38 tucked in the small of my back, which the police quickly seized. Both crooks also had weapons seized, and the three of us were arrested and thrown into the paddy wagon that conveniently awaited us.

I was the last one tossed in the wagon but managed a moment to inform an officer that I was a DEA agent. His response was not reassuring, as the officers continued to toss me into the wagon. I was driven downtown in the wagon and segregated, with me placed in the bullpen – a holding area for arrestees prior to processing.

In that small, confined space with 20 criminals, I was concerned that one of them might recognize me and decide to take matters into their own hands. After what felt like an eternity,

☆ ☆

I was brought to processing, fingerprinted, and photographed. With each officer, I reiterated that I was a DEA agent working undercover and asked to be locked up in segregation.

I was relieved when I found myself in a private cell with an iron bed at around 10 p.m. Around 4 a.m., the night shift commander came to my cell, apologized for the incident, and informed me that I was free to go. He also mentioned that my surveillance team was at a bar we typically hung out at after deals and wanted me to meet with them. I asked for a squad to drop me off, and they accommodated me.

Upon reaching the bar, which should have been closed but stayed open awaiting my arrival, it didn't take me long to join them with what ended up being quite an evening! I then learned the back story behind the arrest and the drive-by shooting and Milwaukee Police surveillance. Back then, different units of the police department seldom communicated, and the detective bureau failed to contact the narcotics bureau before converging on me and the two crooks.

I found out from the surveillance team that after they saw the police department converging on the car I was in; they didn't want to expose the fact that I was working undercover. Additionally, they knew I would be physically safe in the hands of the police department. The Resident Agent in Charge of the Milwaukee office immediately got on the phone to the police department but was unable to get me released without the chief of police's approval.

Finally, the agent in charge went to the police department, provided identification and cleared the way for me to be released. In a relatively brief period, I had an informant tell two crooks that I was a DEA agent in the middle of an attempt to make a buy. Not long after, I was arrested for carrying a concealed-

weapon charge by the Milwaukee Police Department, thrown in a bullpen and then in jail. *Undercover work must be more glamorous than this!*

I got home early later that morning after being released from jail and after leaving the bar, took the rest of the day off.

16

The Birth Of The Cartels and Their Impact On Middle America

In the world of drug investigations, apprehending dealers on their initial transactions is a rarity. As the ensuing case illustrated, dealers outmaneuver law enforcement, conducting numerous transactions unbeknownst to the police. Although not known by law enforcement, after the above marijuana deal, another group was establishing itself as the premier marijuana smuggling organization in the United States. A formidable tentacle of this group existed right under my nose.

A large amount of the marijuana shipped from Colombia in 1977, 1978, and part of 1979 found its way to Burlington, Wisconsin, a stone's throw from the Milwaukee DEA office. *Post-factum* evidence gathering led the IRS and me to initiate a historical conspiracy investigation in early 1979, a laborious process demanding meticulous reconstruction of past transactions and associated crimes.

In 1978, I was working an informant who unveiled a tale of a group in Burlington, Wisconsin, smuggling massive amounts of marijuana from Florida. The informant's details were

substantial enough to prompt an investigation by the IRS and me. Our first in-depth collaboration involved sifting through telephone toll statements and conducting criminal background investigations. IRS had also developed a source who provided similar information.

Upon completing criminal background checks and analyzing telephone toll information, we agreed that an investigation was warranted. This commitment entailed a year or two of collaboration with various law enforcement agencies, coordination efforts, and sacrifices of weekends and holidays. The deeper we got into the case, the greater the chance of undercover penetration and prolonged surveillance.

Collaborating with the Kenosha County Sheriff's Department, the Walworth County Sheriff's Department, the Racine County Sheriff's Department, and the Lake County Illinois Sheriff's Department, we enlisted their help to conduct criminal record checks on the individuals identified by the informant. We sought to identify other possible co-conspirators and determine the hierarchy of the conspiracy.

As the local departments delved into their respective investigations, we witnessed a clearer picture emerging regarding the individuals involved in the conspiracy, both at the top and bottom. The telephone call records identified several people as definite members of the core conspiracy.

IRS typically utilized grand jury proceedings for investigations, while during that time, DEA was more focused on undercover work and short-term investigations. So, unable to find inroads working undercover, we initiated the investigation using grand jury subpoenas. A grand jury, composed of citizens meeting in secret, would listen to evidence presented by witnesses developed by the investigators. The United States attorney would

issue subpoenas requiring people to appear before the grand jury and testify.

These individuals, identified as members of the conspiracy, faced the choice of testifying or being compelled to testify. If they refused to testify, the U.S. attorney would apply for immunity, compelling the witness to testify. However, if the witness still refused, jail awaited until cooperation was granted.

DEA's job as investigators was to identify witnesses, align them with intelligence information, and link them to the conspiracy. The evidence linking them to the conspiracy could be witnesses, a variety of different record information, surveillance conducted by the case agents or undercover buys.

After accumulating a significant amount of intelligence information on potential co-conspirators, and with input from local law enforcement, Harry and I hit the streets. Knocking on doors, conducting surveillance, and engaging in garbage pickups, we aimed to bolster the case and provide the U.S. attorney's office with pertinent questions for the grand jury witnesses.

Several individuals were subpoenaed to testify. After some were granted immunity and others volunteered to testify, a case began evolving—by far the most significant one I had worked on to date. Delving deeper into the case, it became apparent that individuals from Fort Lauderdale were involved as sources of supply. We then began coordinating their efforts with a prosecutor and agent from the Fort Lauderdale DEA office.

In a significant turn of events during July of 1978, many of the main co-conspirators we had identified in our investigation gathered at a motel in Fort Lauderdale. While a bunch of guys meeting in a motel room might not normally raise suspicions, the hundreds of phone calls coming to and going from the room prompted the motel's switchboard to reach its limit. A vigilant

motel employee called the police department, alerting them to suspicious activities.

Responding swiftly, the Fort Lauderdale Police Department dispatched units to establish surveillance on the motel room. They confirmed an unusual amount of traffic, individuals carrying briefcases or suitcases. A decision was made to tail one of the guys leaving the hotel room.

Shortly after, he was stopped at Fort Lauderdale Airport about to board a Learjet, found in possession of $100,000. Several other individuals stopped, each carrying a substantial quantity of currency. One of the individuals stopped actually ended up being an informant on a case several years later. He just happened to be carrying $10,000 in cash when stopped by the police.

The officers, acting on the suspicious activities reported by the motel employee, swiftly entered the motel room. To their astonishment, approximately seven pounds of cocaine and a little over a million dollars in cash were laid out before them.

Unfortunately for the occupants, detailed financial ledgers were also discovered—clear evidence of large drug transactions involving tens of millions of dollars and tons of marijuana. The ledgers even revealed the names of cities where the marijuana was delivered and the cash that was received. Ironically, many of these cities were soon to be revealed as having ongoing active investigations, albeit uncoordinated. Harry had the foresight to contact a Ft. Lauderdale police officer and was able to obtain copies of the financial records that were seized in the motel room. Harry heard about the arrest on a local radio program while driving to work one morning. The name of a local dealer was mentioned as being involved at the motel and that was all Harry needed to jump start the investigation.

Not long after, in September 1978, I found myself once again summoned to Washington D.C. Alongside agents and police officers from across the country. I participated in a meeting involving about 20 different federal and local law enforcement agencies. Independently, all the participants identified tentacles of the organization headquartered in Ft. Lauderdale.

This multi-day meeting facilitated introductions among all involved officers and agents providing contact numbers for efficient communication. This network also allowed law enforcement to collaborate seamlessly, ensuring that all leads were directed to agents actively working on this specific case. An agent was appointed not only to investigate the Fort Lauderdale end of the case but also to handle any issues arising in individual investigations.

To streamline coordination, the tentacles were inserted into one big basket called CENTAC 20, akin to CENTAC 4, the white cross case. All related investigations were now coordinated, funded, and managed from headquarters. Despite resistance from local supervisors, the success of previous CENTAC operations overcame the petty resistance.

During the headquarters' meeting, each case agent briefed others on the nature of individual cases, offering a comprehensive overview. This glimpse provided a screenshot of an organization controlled out of Fort Lauderdale sprawling across the United States and several continents. The organization distributed hundreds of tons of marijuana, netting hundreds of millions of dollars and accounting for a significant percentage of all marijuana distributed within the United States.

The information shared during this meeting corroborated the size and magnitude of the organization, as recounted by Milwaukee's witnesses. Freighters were anchored off the coasts

of Florida and Massachusetts loaded with marijuana, which was then offloaded onto yachts. The yachts transported the contraband to stash houses, serving as temporary storage until distributors arrived.

A peculiar revelation from evidence in the Wisconsin case indicated that elderly parents of some traffickers would drive motorhomes to Florida, which were then filled with marijuana—approximately 2500 pounds per load but sometimes up to 5000 pounds per load. The motorhomes were then driven back to Wisconsin for marijuana distribution.

Another revelation from the headquarters meeting shed light on the organization's handling of immense amounts of cash. Learjets were rented to transport this substantial wealth throughout the country to homes in Southern Florida. The magnitude of the operation was such that a Wisconsin witness shared a curious detail: Instead of counting the money, they would stuff Samsonite suitcases with cash and weigh them, providing a close enough estimate of the money's value. Of course, the scales used to weigh the money were routinely calibrated to be very accurate.

Furthermore, a Wisconsin witness recounted a time when he was charged with guarding a home in Fort Lauderdale that contained a significant amount of money. He estimated that there was between 6 and 10 million dollars in one of the bedrooms, all 100-dollar bills. At some point during his debriefing, I asked him if he ever thought about stealing any of the money. He responded, "I can't steal any of the money because that would be dishonest!"

All I could think was, "Oh my gosh an honest drug dealer!"

17

Not Just A Regular Flight

While working on this case, Harry and I found ourselves flying off to Gillette, Wyoming, hot on the trail of some mules driving RVs loaded with marijuana for the Fort Lauderdale organization. We were trying to develop grand jury witnesses, and the interviews were as routine as they come. Little did we know that our return journey would take an unexpected turn.

As we handed our airplane tickets to the agent, a subtle realization hit—this ticket agent was a guy! In a time when almost all ticket agents were female, it was a minor anomaly, and we didn't think much of it. After flashing our tickets, the agent nonchalantly directed Harry and me to take a seat in the terminal, promising an imminent announcement about the flight.

Suddenly, the agent vanished. Moments later, a voice echoed through the terminal, signaling the green light for boarding. Harry and I followed suit, stepping onto the tarmac. Our eyes widened as we witnessed the male ticket agent loading baggage into an unbelievably small plane.

Seated in our cramped quarters, we heard the captain's voice crackle over the intercom, welcoming everyone aboard

with the standard spiel. But as the flight ascended to cruising altitude, a surprising announcement rippled through the cabin— refreshments on the way. Our curiosity heightened when no stewardess appeared in the minuscule 10 or 12-seater plane.

Then, the curtains of the cockpit parted, revealing the same guy who had handed us our boarding passes and loaded our baggage. Shockingly, he was not just the pilot but also the flight attendant! With a nonchalant demeanor, he pushed a red Coleman cooler into the cabin, urging us to help ourselves. As he retreated to the cockpit, he assured all aboard he would continue flying the plane to Denver. Of course, for the benefit of the individuals on the flight, everybody suspected that somebody else was in the cockpit flying the plane.

Taking a step back to the group of dealers who had been interrupted by the police at the motel, Donald Steinberg, who was sitting in the motel room with cocaine, money, and drug ledgers revealing an incredibly large organization, was arrested and posted bond the next day. Of course, he didn't show up for court and became a fugitive.

To keep the drugs, the money, and the drug ledgers in the same location was a huge violation of the rules of drug dealing. Steinberg provided a fake name and became a fugitive that threw a kink into the plan of arresting everybody involved in the conspiracy at the same time. The specific details of the arrests that occurred at the motel took some time to filter down to the agents who worked on the individual cases throughout the country. Harry's foresight gave us a head start when he directly contacted the Ft. Lauderdale police.

Instead of setting a precise date and time for mass arrests, each conspiracy was allowed to be terminated at the most relevant time for the individual jurisdictions investigating this

case. Because of the unfortunate circumstances involving the escape of the primary defendant, the Milwaukee case went to a grand jury where three of the primary defendants were indicted on numerous charges and arrested. Two of the primary defendants in the Wisconsin case pled guilty in September of 1981 to 12 counts each of drug and tax offenses.

One of the defendants in the Wisconsin case admitted to offloading yachts one to four times a week, over a two-year period with each offload ranging from 10,000 to 12,000 pounds of marijuana. These offloads all occurred in Fort Lauderdale. Also discovered during this investigation was that the marijuana organization spent over one million dollars to rent Learjets every year. The Learjets were used to fly all over the country to pick up Samsonite suitcases full of money from the mid-level dealers.

These Learjets were used to transfer money from various customers in different parts of the United States to stash houses in Fort Lauderdale. Several additional defendants in the Wisconsin case pled guilty and were sentenced to either probation or short times in jail. Drug or money seizures did not occur because the organization stopped delivering marijuana after the motel arrests in Ft. Lauderdale.

It was unfortunate for the Wisconsin agents that we were unable to catch the Wisconsin dealers while they were going full steam ahead. In the end, several of the Wisconsin defendants testified and offered to testify in some of the Fort Lauderdale cases.

Their proffered evidence provided ammunition for the Fort Lauderdale U.S. attorney's office who ended up convicting all the principal defendants. The main Fort Lauderdale source of supply and the head of the organization, Donald Steinberg, was finally arrested in Los Angeles during March of 1981 and sentenced to

prison. James Bell, a lieutenant for Steinberg was convicted after a jury trial and Herman Holbek and Ronald Wesinger, two of the main distribution managers in Wisconsin, pled guilty. Neil Saari developed a case related to the Steinberg case on an individual by the name of John Kramer who over a period of about twenty months bought 3 ½ million dollars of marijuana from Holbach. Kramer was convicted and sentenced to five years in prison. Over time the $100 million dollars in annual revenue generated by his smuggling empire vanished as did his mansions, yachts, luxury cars and co-conspirators.

18

Moving On

Around the time the Fort Lauderdale case was reaching its conclusion, Harry and I decided to shake the trees and see what might fall out. We initiated this by reaching out to our contacts in law enforcement within the eastern Wisconsin region to see if any drug dealers were out there that merited IRS and DEA's attention.

DEA/IRS initial discussions with contacts in law enforcement agencies located in southeastern Wisconsin revealed an intriguing development; it seemed that with the cessation of activities by the Fort Lauderdale group, a new faction had emerged in a county just south of Milwaukee. This new group was actively involved in the distribution of significant quantities of cocaine and marijuana.

Harry and I had already established very strong connections with the agencies we contacted, who readily accepted our offer to join forces with them to see what could be done. The agencies involved provided us with the names of most of the conspirators. Then it was the same old story; background checks, telephone checks, and calls to the informants in the area by DEA/IRS.

Without any formal agreement between any of the agencies or investigators assigned to this case, including DEA and IRS,

the information would be readily shared to see if it could be developed further. During these investigations, Harry and I became close to two officers with whom we had previously worked and developed a rapport: a captain and an officer in a local county sheriff's drug unit. It didn't hurt that we got along with the cities Chief of Police very well.

A brighter picture formed regarding the organization and its structure without even conducting an interview. I had an informant who acknowledged that he was aware of many participants in the drug scheme and could probably convince one of them to sell him some drugs. The informant was also aware that a very large shipment of marijuana was due to be offloaded on the East Coast in the very near future, and a prominent dealer in the new conspiracy was involved with this ship.

During September of 1979, unknown to DEA/IRS, a ship floating off the coast of North Carolina offloaded 36,000 pounds of marijuana as was elicited during a subsequent trial that this load was being managed by Robert Picollo. After being moved from stash houses to vehicles, the load was eventually delivered to Dan Muhlenberg in Wisconsin, one of the primary dealers in this specific case. The load was distributed throughout southeastern Wisconsin and northern Illinois. This load has been referred to as the Hurricane David load.

Unbeknownst to the Milwaukee investigators, in March 1980, another ship named *Captain Tom* had mechanical problems and was abandoned and adrift in the Atlantic Ocean before it was seized by North Carolina investigators. Those investigators ran all the names associated with *Captain Tom* through the DEA database and discovered that one of Milwaukee's prime suspects was deeply involved in the *Captain Tom* investigation. Thirty-six thousand pounds of marijuana destined for all parts

of the United States including Wisconsin were seized because of *Captain Tom's* misfortunes. In later developments it turned out that Picollo and a guy name Billy Breen were managing this load.

Until we realized that the *Captain Tom* incident in North Carolina was related to the current investigation, we continued marching, interviewing witnesses, conducting surveillance, conducting garbage pickups and trying to find some undercover inroads into the new investigation.

Fortunately, we had established good reputations throughout not only the law enforcement community but also throughout the defense bar. Additionally, the United States Attorney's Office for the Eastern District of Wisconsin had a pristine reputation for honesty and integrity which also helped in converting dealers to witnesses. Many of the witnesses to whom Harry and I spoke, agreed to cooperate and testify if granted immunity.

During the summer of 1980, an informant approached us and told us that he could set up two guys with connections to the current case with a small cocaine deal. These two guys were dealing right in the backyard of the principles in the new case so it was assumed, and rightfully so, that they could provide additional information on the new case.

We decided to proceed with the quarter pound cocaine deal. Normally a quarter pound of cocaine during this time would not have generated much interest except for the potential of future witnesses. It didn't take long to have two guys and a quarter pound of cocaine in custody. The deal went as smooth as silk and generated two more witnesses to testify against some of the principal co-conspirators.

Toward the end of 1980, significant inroads were made into identifying and gathering evidence on the principal defendants. The word also was clearly spreading throughout southeastern

Wisconsin, just as it had during the Fort Lauderdale investigation, that there was plenty of heat on these dealers and that people had to start making hard choices: cooperate with the government or go to jail.

My instinctive approach in dealing with law enforcement personnel outside of DEA was always personal. It wasn't as though this was a strategy, but merely a natural part of my makeup. Throughout my career, I naturally gravitated toward forging friendships with individuals in the field: federal judges, magistrates, U.S. attorneys, assistant U.S. attorneys, county sheriffs and deputies, state narcotic agents, and local policemen from various regions.

This trend consistently played out as I traveled for work or leisure, attending weddings, funerals, and frequently bonding over post-drug deal gatherings at taverns. These relationships which formed over the years endured to the present. (I never really became friends with judges or magistrates but always had a very cordial relationship with them.)

My collaborative nature did not shield me from making adversaries within law enforcement circles. This was a consequence of the steadfast and unwavering positions taken during investigations. That stubbornness was not always the right call as far as relations with other agencies, but most of the time it was. A notable instance involved a local county sheriff's department proposing an operation based on intelligence suggesting that prominent Mexican drug dealers gathered at a specific bar every Friday night.

Despite the pressure to support or participate in the surveillance, I stood firm, asserting my conviction that drug dealers don't adhere to such predictable patterns. If I supported such a useless endeavor, it would be a tremendous waste of

manpower and money that could be used for more productive cases. I understood the officer in charge had a penchant for wild goose chases, and, true to form, this endeavor turned out to be just that. I would have been much more popular in this case as well as others if I had gone with the flow.

On the other side of the coin, there were many more occasions for which I worked and developed both professional and personal friendships with law enforcement officers outside of DEA. Taking a back seat to a local police agency or other federal police agency was not an obstacle for me and I actually enjoyed watching how they approached a problem both in similar ways and in different ways as DEA. I learned pretty early on that there was a huge difference between arrogance and experience. Experience would always rub off and become much more powerful than arrogance.

During December of 1980, three of the suspects related to the *Captain Tom* case contacted a Pasco County Florida sheriff through an informant regarding the purchase of a thousand pounds of marijuana. DEA /IRS were eventually contacted and were requested to conduct a file check on these three dealers and of course they were identified as being deeply involved in the *Captain Tom* conspiracy. The Pasco County Sheriff's Office contacted either Harry or I indicating there was a possibility of a reverse undercover operation in Florida.

A reverse undercover deal is when law enforcement in an undercover capacity act as if the police are the dealers selling the drugs to the real drug dealers. After all the i's were dotted and t's crossed, Don, a detective from a local police department, and I took a trip to Florida and met some real good policemen. Of course, Harry met us in Pasco County.

Because Harry, Don and I were the invited guests of the Pasco County Sheriff's Department, we took a back seat and got

to observe the deal occur at arm's length. We could tell that the Pasco County deputies were appreciative of the Wisconsin guys not trying to strong arm the case.

After preparations were made for the surveillance and arrests to be conducted at the appropriate time, one of the Pasco County Deputy sheriffs pulled me aside and told me that their undercover officer was extremely experienced and could do a deal like this standing on his head with a couple of Wisconsin hicks. That was a signal to Harry and me that the Pasco County guys, and the Wisconsin guys were going to get along just fine.

Arrangements were made for a meeting between the Wisconsin dealers and the Pasco County deputy during which time the deputy showed the Wisconsin dealers a thousand pounds of marijuana. One of the Wisconsin dealers produced a little more than $100,000 and indicated that he would produce another $100,000 after he sold the marijuana. Obviously, things didn't get that far, and the Wisconsin dealers were arrested right after they showed the $100,000.

The Wisconsin detective, Harry, and I interviewed all the guys that got arrested and found them to be more than willing to assist law enforcement in the Wisconsin investigation. Harry and my colleagues' laid-back position with Pasco County deputies on the execution of the drug deal paid off in aces. It turned out that the Pasco County undercover deputy had been doing these reverse undercover cases for several years after Colombian marijuana arrived.

When the arrest went down, the four or five defendants were transported back to Pasco County. A sergeant explained to the Wisconsin dealers the importance of them cooperating and how things ran a little bit differently in Pasco County, Florida, then up north. The sergeant made his point.

Three of the arrestees were debriefed which shined a much brighter light on the overall conspiracy including some new names of higher echelon dealers/sources of supply. Additionally, the information gained provided relatively accurate dates and places where deals involving the rest of the conspirators occurred. They provided us with a lot more evidence but also a lot more work to be done to corroborate their proposed testimony.

We returned to Wisconsin with our feet on the ground and ready to interview additional witnesses. We now had significant new facts to back up our interviews. Harry and I knew that word had gotten out to the Wisconsin dealers regarding the arrest that had just gone down in Pasco County. We also knew that the ante of poker had just gone up for the dealers that remained on the street.

The remaining conspirators in Wisconsin were now in a position of wondering whether one, two or three of the guys arrested in Pasco County had flipped and were working with the government. The paranoia was intense, and everybody would be looking in every direction trying to figure out when the hammer was going to fall. Just as important, the dealers still working the streets were also wondering who they could talk to, who they could deal with, and even who they could associate with for fear of getting swept up.

The Pasco County guys made our job a lot easier, and now it was just a matter of interviewing the co-conspirators that we thought would be the most productive for the case. In some cases, we re-interviewed co-conspirators who had previously told us to pound sand because they knew we were fishing. At this point in time, it was pretty much assumed on the street that the government knew everything, and that if we showed up at their door, they only had one choice. As difficult a choice as it

was, many of the conspirators that we interviewed thought the government was a much better option than jail.

It really put a different perspective on an interview when agents knew we got the irrefutable facts on our side and the only option for the interviewee was to lie, lawyer up, or give it up. Fortunately for the good guys (or depending on one's point of view, the bad guys) most of the people we targeted for interviews either gave it up or hired attorneys. Several of the attorneys hired by the future witnesses had previous interactions with Harry and me either in court or debriefings and knew that we didn't fool around and always shot accurately and straight.

As a result, within several months most of our evidence had been gathered, and we had a very strong case to present to the U.S. attorney's office. Throughout the whole investigation, the U.S. attorney's office was kept informed as to the general details of the case but now we were able to get into specific facts that were corroborated by the evidence in the case. We also, during the post Pasco County interviews, identified a source of supply for marijuana from Georgia, a guy named Billy Breen and another source of supply for cocaine and marijuana in Miami, Tania Martinez. Breen was one of the main guys in both the Hurricane David and Capt. Tom marijuana smuggling ventures.

During about May of 1981, one of the mid-level dealers in the Wisconsin case offered an informant 20 pounds of marijuana for sale. Knowing that if we arrested this guy with 20 pounds, he would likely provide us with additional information. Arrangements were made for the meeting and the guy was arrested, 20 pounds of marijuana was seized, and we had another witness this time further up the ladder. It was an uneventful arrest.

All three of the dealers, possessing 4 ounces of cocaine and 20 pounds of marijuana, arrested during the summers of 1980

and 1981, knew before they did the deals that there was plenty of heat going around, but like so many that had preceded them, they thought they were smarter than the police.

On both deals, however, when the informants were negotiating with the dealers, it was decided by both parties to do the transactions closer to Milwaukee because of all the heat. That was fine with DEA/IRS because it was a shorter prisoner transport to jail. As anticipated based on solid confirmed intelligence, the dealer of the 20 pounds of marijuana and the two dealers of four ounces of cocaine both flipped and ended up cooperating after their uneventful arrests.

Neither of the two arrests went unnoticed by the principal co-conspirators who had yet to meet either Harry or me or the policeman working with us. Things progressed rapidly after about 12 to 16 months of working on the case. However as with most cases, a political twist occurred with the marijuana source of supply that we could not untwist.

During November of 1981, the source of supply for the four ounces of cocaine mentioned above, was charged with one count of distribution and one count of conspiracy. He agreed to plead guilty. We were certainly moving in the right direction at this point. As a matter of fact, we were now playing with a stacked deck of cards, and the few dealers that had not stepped forward were beginning to think hard about it.

Also, during November of 1981, five of the principal defendants, through their attorneys, initiated plea bargains with the U.S. attorney's office. Not long after the above, five dealers entered guilty pleas in the Eastern District of Wisconsin for various violations of the Controlled Substances Act.

All five waived their right to have their cases heard before a grand jury and negotiated their punishment with individual plea

agreements. Before they were allowed to plead guilty, each of them sat down with Harry and me and unburdened themselves. If there were any inconsistencies in their stories, the facts that we had gathered significantly refreshed their memories.

This was noteworthy because by waving the right to indictment, they basically admitted that the cases against them were provable beyond a reasonable doubt. That was not as significant as the message that was sent to the other co-defendants who had not yet faced reality and continued their lives as if nothing was happening, except the paranoia which was brewing inside each of them. After seeing five of their buddies pleading guilty to federal felonies, I could only imagine the stress that they endured by not jumping on the bandwagon.

Between the summer of 1981 and the fall of 1981, while we were putting together additional evidence gathered or seized during our investigation, an agent from Atlanta belonging to another federal agency showed up in the Milwaukee office wanting to talk to the Resident Agent in Charge. Before they began their conversation, the agent in charge called Harry and me into his office so we could participate in what was anticipated to be a contentious meeting. DEA Milwaukee had been hearing whispers that they might be getting a visit from a sometimes-hostile agency.

The first thing that I noticed was that the unexpected agent was wearing a Wyatt Earp holster containing some kind of large handgun. As expected, he indicated that the guy we had identified as the primary source of supply for marijuana, Billy Breen, needed to walk from his charges. In layman's terms, he wanted the primary source of supply in the Wisconsin case not to be charged at all. He further indicated that he couldn't provide much more information than that. This turn of events was totally expected.

I had a few questions that deserved an answer. Why in hell should he be trusted when he wouldn't answer any of the basic questions we had for him? He clearly didn't trust us. Not unusual at all. The second question—Why should Milwaukee turn a blind eye on a guy who was the main source of supply of marijuana for southeastern Wisconsin? The third—Why didn't Harry and I get the customary telephone call from him giving us a heads up that he was coming to Milwaukee? More importantly—What interest did he have in coming to Milwaukee? This Atlanta agent oozed unfettered arrogance.

Harry and I handled situations such as the above completely differently. Harry remained completely professional and as a good undercover agent would, pretended to go along with the game that was being played. I on the other hand generally resisted sometimes using unprofessional terms especially if I felt I was being played. I couldn't recall specifically what he said or did at the conclusion of this meeting but based on a long history of interagency games, I was not very subtle.

Of course, both Harry and I and the Resident Agent in Charge advised that the target we were talking about was extremely important to an ongoing investigation. Of course, Wyatt Earp's investigation was much more important than Milwaukee's investigation. Harry was cordial enough with him but indicated that if he wasn't willing to provide more information, we would have to think hard about Wyatt's proposal. I already said enough.

On this trip or a follow-up trip, a friend of mine in the U.S. attorney's office indicated that the Wyatt Earp guy had paid a visit to the U.S. attorney's office. It was at this time when we realized that Milwaukee might be in trouble and risked losing the biggest fish we had in our pond. The reason behind this potential nightmare was that it was customary for a visiting agent from

any outfit to coordinate meetings with outside agencies with the agents with whom he was working directly.

As silently as Wyatt Earp agent had come into Milwaukee, he left just the same. Harry and I did decide however to have Wyatt's witness come to Milwaukee for a meeting with him. Did I forget to mention that Breen was looking at a substantial amount of time in prison in the Wisconsin case. Harry and I assumed and rightfully so that the witness/defendant had been working on the side trying to make a buck but got caught up in Milwaukee's' case involving all the Wisconsin dealers.

Shortly afterwards, I got a surprise call from the administrator of the DEA, not long after agent Wyatt Earp's first trip to Milwaukee. The administrator congratulated me on the case we had assembled against the Wisconsin violators and their sources of supply. He also thanked me for working with the other agency and encouraged me to continue cooperating because of the importance of the case Wyatt Earp guy was involved in. I asked him if he could divulge any information regarding the secret case, and he very cordially declined. We would soon find out about the secret case.

19

Witness/Informant/ Drug Dealer

It was no easy chore to identify exactly what type of witness/ informant Breen was. He was in fact both a witness, an informant and a dealer. Witnesses in drug cases were typically individuals who got caught up in the drug trade, arrested and decided to testify against the other participants in their scheme. In most cases witnesses were not proactive, meaning that they were not actively participating in or attempting to set up other dealers for law enforcement. They had already done that.

Informants on the other hand came in many different colors. Before informants were utilized, they needed to be screened very carefully by interviewing law enforcement officers to determine what their motivation was. Some informants approached law enforcement because they were good citizens and observed a bad thing. Some informants were individuals who had been arrested and actively attempted to set up the dealers they were associated with to have them arrested by law enforcement.

Some dealers became informants simply for financial gain. They received a monetary award for the quality of the drug dealer and the amount of drugs seized by law enforcement.

Some individuals involved in the drug trade became informants to make money from law enforcement or to make money doing deals on the side without law enforcement's knowledge. Some individuals did it because of a grudge. There were several other types of informants, but Breen fit in all the above categories apart from being a good citizen doing the right thing.

Sometimes Breen offered criminals to his law enforcement handlers strictly for the financial reward. Sometimes he would offer the criminals up because of grudges, and sometimes he would offer them up only after he got caught committing a crime without the knowledge of law enforcement. That was an example of how Breen used law enforcement to his advantage. Sometimes he got caught and gave up everybody he was committing the crime with, and sometimes he didn't get caught and made a bunch of money.

Just as there were many different types of informants, there were many different types of law enforcement officers who approached and evaluated informants. Unfortunately, there were law enforcement officers who believed everything their informants told them. Breen was a master manipulator who was arranging crimes for his own profit and at the same time telling law enforcement about crimes, again for profit or legal consideration. A difficult informant to say the least. It also can't be denied that Breen made some good cases for law enforcement around the country. It also can't be denied Breen committed a crime or two under the radar.

The night finally came for his arrival in Milwaukee. His arrival was arranged by the agent from Atlanta, and Harry and I, suspicious of both Wyatt Earp's motivation and Breen's motivation, were skeptical. It didn't take long to figure out that his current motivation was nothing more than getting out of a jam.

As soon as he got into my OGV (official government vehicle), I could tell that he had been around the block once or twice. On the way to a local bar, we played the typical head games that guys like Billy and agents like me played with each other, kind of like sticking our toe in the water and seeing if it's cold or warm. I was cold, and Billy was uncommonly confident and cocky. He also gave me the impression that he was here to help, and that I should be thankful for his generous cooperation.

Billy either didn't know how much trouble he was in, or Wyatt Earp had failed to inform him that he was in a 'boat load' of trouble. The other possibility was, and fortunately for Billy, his value to the government had been sold to and bought by the higher-ups of both DEA and Wyatt Earp's agency. I never let him know how much bargaining power he had because of course I didn't know what his value was.

Breen seemed to have a mix of Southern Charm and New York wise guy blended in his personality. He didn't have any problem bragging about all the valuable work he had done for the United States government. He also let me know that he was a very important component of the Wisconsin case and would have very important disclosures to make when he was debriefed.

I assured him that the government knew exactly what his involvement was in the Wisconsin case, and that there was no sense in him trying to either maximize or minimize his role because we had just about all the facts. I was surprised at his minimal reaction "Whatever." This of course caught me off guard because I was fairly impressed with the amount of information that had been gathered over the months regarding his involvement in the whole Wisconsin group of guys.

The only conclusion I could draw was that the Atlanta agent had prepared him for our meeting and further had assured

him that things would be handled just as they had always been. Breen's role in the Wisconsin case and the *Captain Tom* case was that of a manager. As the *Captain Tom* was sailing north with its cargo of 36,000 pounds of marijuana, Breen was making sure stash houses had been arranged, cars had been rented, payment had been arranged and transportation finalized.

The only thing missing in the whole equation was that Billy forgot to tell Wyatt Earp what was going on with the *Captain Tom* load of marijuana. And of course, Breen had also put himself in a position to turn on a dime in case he felt any heat from the *Captain Tom* endeavor. He learned from years on the street and in prison how to manipulate, calculate and when called for, to extricate. He always had a back door to escape justice, Wyatt Earp being the key to the lock. That's exactly what happened while he was in Milwaukee and when he left Milwaukee. As in all cases with informants who were working the system, hindsight was admittedly a lot easier than real-time evaluation.

Although Harry and I were dragged through the process kicking and screaming, common sense told us that we had to leave this one alone and give up on it. We had no chance of convincing DEA, IRS, the Department of Justice or Wyatt Earp and his agency that Billy Breen should go to prison for a long time.

While in Milwaukee, Breen did provide significant evidence which corroborated the many witnesses they already had lined up. He did add several tidbits which we were not aware of, one of which was that an additional 36,000-pound load of marijuana arrived on the East Coast at about the time Hurricane David was roaring its ugly head during September 1979. The marijuana had been driven from North Carolina to Wisconsin and delivered to Danny, one of the Racine ringleaders, and his associates.

After the 36,000 pounds of marihuana was sold, Billy came to Wisconsin to collect his end of the proceeds. He was carrying about 1.5 million dollars that he had collected from Danny. While at O'Hare Airport, he decided to stuff the money in his clothing and had just about accomplished the task when he realized if he stuffed anymore, it would look abnormal. He figured the best way to get away looking halfway normal was to flush $20,000 down one of the toilets at the airport. He admitted this without hesitation.

In the end, he cut sweetheart deals with the United States attorney's office in Milwaukee and with the District Attorney's office in New Brunswick, North Carolina, where *Captain Tom* became disabled. It wasn't until several years later that I finally figured out why he was such a hot commodity and deserving of such gentle treatment. As bait, he did tell me the last three names of some allegedly very important criminals involved in very big crimes: Kelly, Kearns and Margeson.

The crimes which led to his sweetheart deals were the attempted assassination of a prominent and well-regarded assistant United States attorney and the actual assassination of the United States court district judge from the same judicial district. Billy had a guy who was interested in killing someone, and he also had a guy who was willing for the right price to assassinate the unknown target.

What Billy didn't know was that the subject of the assassination was in fact an assistant United States attorney. This prosecutor was highly respected and very aggressive on drug cases. On that fateful day, the assassin pumped round after round into the AUSA's vehicle but fortunately failed in his mission, wounding the government attorney. That was about November 1978.

Reviewing the evidence of the attempted assassination of the assistant United States attorney and the *Captain Tom* shipwreck, he was connected to two of the schemes.

He was one of the principal players in putting the *Captain Tom* smuggling scheme together along with his partner in that venture, Bobby Picollo. Picollo was subsequently sentenced to a lengthy term in the North Carolina prison system for the *Captain Tom* case.

Looking back, Picollo approached Breen to see if he knew anybody who could pull off a big job. Picollo was a close associate of Jimmy Chagra who was being investigated by the assistant United States attorney mentioned above. Not knowing what the job was, Breen simply said that he could in fact find somebody to pull off a big job but didn't want to know anything about it after it was done.

He put Picollo together with James Kearns, one of the three guys he mentioned to me while in Milwaukee. Not long after that introduction, the attempt was made on the assistant United States attorney's life. Because it was a failed attempt, Picollo was not happy with Breen's recommendation of Kearns because the attempted hit was unsuccessful.

Unfortunately, during May of 1979, an assassin killed a federal district judge. It took a single bullet to take the life of a man who dedicated himself to justice. The common thread between the attempted assassination of the assistant United States attorney and the successful assassination of the federal district judge was a drug smuggler who was about to stand trial in front of the judge. The common thread was Chagra, a close associate of Picollo who was the partner of Breen in the marijuana smuggling cases.

Chagra relied on Picollo to find somebody to hit the assistant United States attorney, and Picollo turned to Breen who recommended Kearns. Because of the failed attempt on the life of the assistant United States attorney, Chagra began scouting on another hit man for the federal judge. Believe it or not, he met him on a golf course in Las Vegas and hired him immediately. Although the hit was successful, it occurred just before Chagra was to appear before the judge on a drug trial.

Ultimately justice caught up with Chagra who was sentenced to 30 years in federal prison after being convicted, during April of 1980, of participating in a Continuing Criminal Enterprise, in violation of 21 USC 848. Chagra was, to say the least, a significant drug dealer and overall vicious criminal. Additionally, during June of 1984, Chagra entered a plea of guilty for plotting to kill the assistant United States attorney. Earlier Chagra pled guilty to an obstruction of justice charge in relation to the murder of the federal judge and was sentenced to life in prison.

One month later Kearns pled guilty to conspiracy to kill the assistant United States attorney, and he too was sentenced to life in prison.

20

Moving Back to the Racine Case

Although Harry, Neil Saari and I had done significant damage to the Wisconsin operation, and the North Carolina authorities had done significant damage on their end, there were two more pieces of the puzzle to put together. The first, Peter Whorley, was a significant part of the Wisconsin organization. But as things ended, he still had not been indicted, although reams of evidence had been gathered against him. In order to move things forward, Neil who was the IRS case agent in charge of the Whorley part of the case and I decided to introduce ourselves and see if they could convince Whorley to capitulate.

Neil placed the telephone call to him, introduced himself, and told him we wanted to meet with him. There was no need to discuss what the meeting involved. Furthermore, Neil told him the meeting would be in his best interest and that this would be his last chance to work out a deal with the government. Much to Neil's surprise, he agreed to a meeting, and a time and a place were set.

Neil and I drove down to meet Whorley at the pre-arranged meeting spot. After we identified ourselves, we told Peter he

didn't have to say anything or answer any questions but just listen very carefully and evaluate the information the way an average citizen seated in a jury box would.

Basically, Whorley was told that the government had volumes of evidence against him and many witnesses who were willing to testify against him. He was provided specific dates, amounts of drugs, and people involved. Based on the evidence, Neil and I told him that we felt he was looking at a Continuing Criminal Enterprise violation which was a 10-year to life sentence.

He was very polite, listening intensely to our offer then matter of factly said, "I'll get an attorney and get in touch."

It wasn't too much longer when an attorney that Neil and I had worked with before on other criminal prosecutions contacted the U.S. attorney's office and struck a deal for Peter. It turned out to be a very good deal opposed to what he would have been looking at if he had taken it to a jury trial. That would have resulted in a sentence of 10 years to life.

During April of 1982, Muhlenberg, Tania Martinez and Peter Whorley were indicted for various violations of both the Controlled Substances Act and violation of various IRS laws.

Muhlenberg was indicted on the Continuing Criminal Enterprise statute which meant he was facing 10 years to life in prison. All the above dealers reached plea agreements with the United States attorney's office. The agreement was for the United States attorney's office to recommend nine years in Muhlenberg's case, seven years in Whorley's case, and five years in Martinez case.

In a move that was certainly unusual, Muhlenberg, Whorley and Martinez were all allowed to move their cases from Milwaukee to Miami where judges were much more lenient. The reason for this was because the cases heard by the Miami judges were so

much bigger in the amounts of drugs than those in Milwaukee. Muhlenberg was sentenced to a 64-month term, Peter Whorley to a 60-month term, and Martinez to an unknown term in federal prison. During Muhlenberg's sentencing, the court considered that he was a Vietnam vet suffering from PTSD.

In the end, a total of 38 drug arrests were made including the Pasco County reverse undercover operation, the *Captain Tom* 36,000 pounds marijuana seizure, the Hurricane David 36,000 pounds and the indictments returned in the Wisconsin case. What this case demonstrated was that if different agencies cooperated and shared information, drug dealers would be the losers and law enforcement and communities the winners. The ultimate accomplishment was that law enforcement cut off the head of a huge marijuana and cocaine-smuggling organization.

At the conclusion of the above investigations, cocaine and marijuana virtually dried up in Southern Wisconsin for a significant period of time. The reason for the success of this case was the willingness of agents and police officers from various agencies and locations throughout the United States to trust each other and work together.

21

The Surveillance From Hell

During the latter half of 1982, when Harry and I were just finishing up with the Wisconsin case, Harry told me that a couple of other IRS agents who I knew and worked well with, had a great informant who could provide significant information. After some back-and-forth, arrangements were made for me to meet with the informant and three IRS agents, Harry and Neil Saari, were two of the agents. At the appointed time and place, I went to a house on Milwaukee's East Side, I met with the three agents and after preliminary agreements were made, met the informant.

Prior to meeting with the informant, I was briefed by the IRS guys. Basically, the IRS had been working on a group of cocaine dealers from a tax perspective with DEA playing a secondary role. The information that the informant had offered the IRS regarded a specific drug deal that the number two man in this organization was going to conduct with a source of supply located in Colorado. The information, if deemed reliable, would require extensive surveillance from Milwaukee to Colorado to observe the transaction and identify the dealer. It was no easy task.

I had been gathering intelligence on the informant for a significant amount of time, although I couldn't find anything to stick. Up until this point my investigation was being conducted independently of the IRS, not for any reason. This was before the informant approached the IRS. Fortunately, the IRS developed a significant tax case against him, enough to make him want to talk to the government.

After I was introduced to the informant, he told the following story. Tony Peters was a very significant cocaine dealer in Milwaukee who was dealing kilos of cocaine, some of which ended up in the hands of very prominent Milwaukeeans. He had a brother, Larry, who worked with him in the drug business.

The informant told us that during the evening of the same day, Larry Peters and a female were going to drive from Milwaukee to Aspen, Colorado, to receive a large quantity of cocaine from Larry's source. This didn't leave much time for planning, so Harry and I put together a team of IRS and DEA agents to first locate and then establish surveillance on Larry to see if he would indeed travel to Aspen. We assembled 4 IRS agents and 2 DEA agents, along with 4 vehicles.

This was not the first time the volunteer agents were told to throw their GO bags in their G cars and get ready to roll. They were also told to call home and let their wives or husbands know that they were leaving for out of town and did not know when they would return. Every agent from both agencies volunteered; subsequently, it was just a matter of picking random agents.

On surveillance like this, DEI (Diversity equity and inclusion) was an important factor because of the different situations that might occur during such a long surveillance. Harry and I picked a black agent, two females and the rest white guys. That way if the dealer stopped en route to the destination, a mixture of colors and genders could be inserted to see what was happening without arousing suspicion.

The surveillance consisted of vehicles all with Wisconsin license plates. The team, consisting of Harry, Neil Saari, three other agents and me, located Larry Peter's vehicle and established surveillance on it, and sure enough at the given time, which was about 6 p.m., Larry and the female got in the car and drove to I-94 west. The whole surveillance team was scratching their heads because very seldom do drug deals happen the way they're supposed to happen.

The team had no problem following Larry out of Milwaukee toward Aspen. Of course, the night dragged on and people were getting tired. About 2:00 in the morning Larry pulled off and rented a motel room. During the short amount of time that he was in the motel room, the agents took turns filling their cars up with gas, getting snacks, going to the washroom, and getting a quick cat nap when they weren't on the point. (The person on the point was the one who had an eye directly on the target vehicle and called out any movement.)

After a couple hours passed, Larry jumped back in the car and started heading west. As we traveled through various DEA jurisdictions, it was protocol for me to contact them and let them know a Milwaukee moving surveillance was in their area with a destination of Aspen. Also, on the way, I contacted the Denver office to let them know that we thought we would be traveling through Denver. None of the notifications seem to pique any interest, so they just kept on following.

Somewhere on the eastern edge of Denver, Larry pulled over and placed a telephone call from a pay phone which was observed by IRS agent Harry. We paid attention to how long he was on the telephone and exactly what time the call was placed, and after

the call ended Larry and his girlfriend left continuing their drive to Aspen. IRS agent Harry went to the pay phone and retrieved the phone number. After he got the number, he broadcast on the radio that he had the number in hand, and he would be rejoining us on our surveillance.

What happened next was a stroke of luck for the Denver office and bad luck for us. The Denver office had been up on what is known as a pen register, which is a device that records any outgoing calls made from a telephone. The individual's phone that the pen register was connected to happened to be a high-level drug trafficker in the Denver area and as it turned out, Denver wanted him really bad.

Denver agents noticed that the telephone number they were monitoring received a phone call at the same time as the phone call IRS agent Harry observed drug dealer Larry place. After the above observation was made, Denver agents quickly determined that Larry from Milwaukee had called the individual whose telephone they were monitoring. The guy who received the phone call was a high-level drug dealer that the Denver DEA had spent many hours working on.

This is where the bad luck for the Milwaukee agents started. The individual whose phone the Denver agents were monitoring was a very significant dealer, and Denver needed just a little bit more evidence so they could plug in and listen to the actual voice calls instead of just recording the numbers. Basically, the phone call that Larry placed gave the Denver DEA Task Force agents additional probable cause to initiate a wiretap investigation, commonly referred to as a T3.

With Milwaukee's information and IRS agent Harry's observation, they had enough to consider a wiretap on one of their primary drug distributors. That also meant that we would

very unlikely be able to stop any drug deal that Larry was about to get involved in. If we did break up the drug deal that was about to happen in Aspen, the Aspen dealer's phone would not be used for any additional drug calls, thereby making the T3 useless. The wind was taken out of the sails of a very tired group of Milwaukee surveillance agents. Selflessly though, each of the agents on the surveillance was disappointed although we understood the big picture and plodded on.

After the phone call, the surveillance team headed up the mountain toward Aspen. The surveillance wasn't that challenging until it started snowing and continued snowing harder. When the snow began, the surveillance vehicles were spaced very far apart, and they relied on the point car to lead. At one point in the surveillance however, it was snowing so hard that Larry stopped his car, and the surveillance vehicles started stacking up directly behind his. An IRS vehicle actually gave Larry a little push when his Larry's vehicle got stuck.

Of course, we all had Wisconsin license plates, but it was snowing so hard that Larry wasn't paying any attention. Because of the traffic jam on the mountain, most occupants of the vehicles got out just to stretch their legs. We even had a moment where one of the DEA surveillance agents, a black agent, walked up to Larry's car and started a conversation with his girlfriend while standing outside the car. A blinding snowstorm, a treacherous mountain road, a group of DEA agents, a drug dealer and a friendly conversation between the dealer and a black DEA agent near Aspen, CO. Hard to believe, but true.

Not being bashful, several other surveillance agents joined in the conversation which was basically about the snowy conditions. It was at this point when I realized that when the dealers made

the stop in the motel a couple hours back, instead of sleeping they snorted cocaine and felt no pain.

If you think about it, only on a snowy mountain road between Aspen and Denver could you find a drug dealer talking to several drug agents in the middle of a snowstorm and in the middle of a dope deal. What was amazing was that to this day Larry never figured out that his newfound friends on the mountain road in the snowstorm were all drug agents!

The surveillance team finally got up to Aspen and observed Larry Park his car. It didn't take long for a male, who had already arrived, to approach Larry's car, open the trunk and place a suitcase in his trunk. Once again super-agent, IRS agent Harry, saw the above activity and reported it on the radio which was overheard by Denver agents. The Denver agents knew as well as the Milwaukee agents that the suitcase was filled with cocaine. What happened next was that Larry and his friend drove the car to the Denver airport, parked, and walked into the terminal catching a flight back to Milwaukee without removing the suitcase from the trunk. Two IRS agents jumped on the same flight to maintain surveillance.

So now a car was sitting in an airport parking lot, with a trunk full of cocaine, and a bunch of very tired agents. After they made sure that Larry and his friend were boarding a flight back to Milwaukee and not returning to the car, we had a drug sniffing dog walk by the trunk, and it immediately alerted us to the presence of a controlled substance.

According to the evidence, Milwaukee agents were following a drug dealer whose goal was to buy cocaine. The drug dealer placed a telephone call to a phone being monitored by DEA Denver and operated by a known drug dealer. A white male placed a suitcase in the trunk. A drug dog alerted agents on the

contents of the trunk of Larry's car. Larry and his friend entered the airport then jumped on a plane heading to Milwaukee with no baggage.

Nothing more needed to be said among the agents because they all knew that wiretaps took precedence over kilogram busts. Hoping that their common sense wouldn't prevail, the team-maintained surveillance on the vehicle parked in the airport parking lot containing the suitcase. That was when IRS agent Harry and I were summoned to meet the Special Agent in Charge (SAC) of the Denver DEA division in a hotel between Aspen and Denver. I of course knew what the meeting was about when told to take no action under any circumstances on the vehicle the team was watching.

When Harry and I got to the hotel, several of the Denver Task Force case agents introduced us to the SAC who provided us with a couple of ice-cold beers. Even though the SAC was not in Milwaukee's chain of command, he still oversaw the Denver area and therefore oversaw the Denver case and its ultimate outcome. Knowing that we had been in our cars for about 24 hours, he let us down as gently as he could but told them he was taking over the case because of the wiretap.

What made the SAC's decision easier to swallow for the Milwaukee team was they could tell by the way he talked that he had been a street agent at one time and understood completely the letdown that the team faced.

The SAC told the team to maintain surveillance on the vehicle in the airport parking lot until his agents could assume those duties. He was gracious and thanked the team for giving his agents the probable cause that they needed to consider a wiretap and listen to their primary defendant distribute his drugs to customers from all over the United States. I notified

the DEA agents, and Harry notified the IRS agents who were all still maintaining surveillance on the car with the suitcase and cocaine in the trunk.

After the Milwaukee agents were relieved, they headed down the mountain back to Milwaukee, still without any sleep. As we got to the outskirts of Denver, I shot into coffee shop and ordered several cups of coffee which I would need for the 17 hour or so return trip to Milwaukee.

What I didn't order and what I didn't need was the hole in the bottom of one of the cups that I placed between my legs. The coffee was really hot! However, I endured and tried to keep up with the convoy of vehicles heading back to Milwaukee. The beers that Harry and I drank with the SAC did not help ease the long drive home, but we all got home safely.

I never asked nor was it ever volunteered what happened to the car in the parking lot or the wiretap in Denver. When I arrived home 17 or 18 hours later, I sat in my driveway and wondered, *What the . . . !*

What did occur after we left Denver was, the DEA Task Force initiated a wiretap on Peter's source of supply, Steve Grabow. The result of that wiretap and one other was the indictment and arrest of Grabow, seven others and the seizure of about $1,000,000 in cash along with other assets. Tragically one month before Grabow's scheduled trial, in December 1985, as he entered his car parked at a posh Aspen club, a car bomb exploded killing Grabow.

22
Summer, 1982

During the summer of 1982 while we were finishing the Wisconsin case, something occurred that would occupy me and others for the next 18 months. Two inmates in the Wisconsin State Prison System agreed that when they got out of prison, they would become partners in the cocaine distribution business. One of the guys, James Brill, was serving 18 months for a drug conviction and the other, Dillard Kelly was serving a sentence for a manslaughter conviction. (A guy was hiding behind a door and knowing that, Dillard pumped three rounds into the door and killed the guy.)

When Kelly and Brill were released from prison during the fall of 1982, Dillard began purchasing quarter pound quantities of cocaine from Brill on a regular basis. Dillard was from the inner city of Milwaukee, and Brill was from the Fox Valley, north of Milwaukee. This arrangement lasted until the fall of 1983 when Dillard met Jose Diaz in Chicago who began to regularly supply Dillard with multi-kilograms of cocaine and who then would resell them to Brill. Not long into this arrangement, Brill cut Dillard out and began dealing directly with the guy from Chicago, Diaz.

At about the same time, the Wisconsin Department of Justice as well as the IRS Criminal Intelligence Division began gathering intelligence on this newly spawned organization. During this time Brill freely discarded his drug notes in his garbage on a weekly basis. Very early in the morning from December of 1983 until August of 1984, a tenacious IRS agent would pick through Brill's garbage on a weekly basis. Almost weekly this agent would discover detailed drug notes identifying Brill's customers, the amount of drugs they were purchasing and the amount they owed.

I eventually met Dillard, but Dillard was using me as insurance, and I was using Dillard for information. He was talking to me so in the event he got busted, he could say that he was working with me to avoid any future charges. What he didn't know was that my experience with informants, especially Billy from the Southern Wisconsin case, prepared me for this type of informant and the games he would play.

When I first met Dillard, I had no idea that he had jumped into the game while he was still in prison. I did know that he murdered a man and had a reputation on the street as being cold and ruthless. I did not complete the proper paperwork for him to be an informant as required by DEA. Instead, I used him strictly to gather intelligence on all types of criminal behavior in Milwaukee's inner city and stayed away from developing an actual criminal case. I was comfortable enough by now that I was confident Dillard would not be able to manipulate me.

As time went on, I found Dillard to be pleasant but conniving. I did everything I could do to prevent him from winning the game of chess we were playing. After several months, I sold him on my fake naivete, and he began to feed me tiny morsels of information, some of which I used or passed on to other law

enforcement agencies. One of the pieces of information involved a guy in Northern Wisconsin by the name of James Brill who according to Dillard was a large-scale cocaine trafficker.

I knew that Dillard gave up Brill's name because Brill had recently jumped the line and started dealing with Jose Diaz from Chicago directly and would no longer deal with Dillard. There was nothing in the world of a drug dealer more offensive than getting cut out of the action which was exactly what happened to Dillard Kelly. What he didn't realize was that he was providing me with information he thought to be innocuous; however, I used it to develop a pretty good picture of Brill's organization.

Not long after starting to work with Dillard, I began receiving information from informants and other law enforcement agencies that Dillard was back in the business selling cocaine. He was doing exactly what I anticipated, so I needed to make a decision about my future. I set up a meeting with him at a restaurant on the northside of downtown Milwaukee. Dillard was right on time as usual and after exchanging pleasantries, I told him we needed to talk.

I cut right to the chase and told him about the information I had been receiving and that if he couldn't guarantee that he would get out of the business, we would have to end our agent/informant relationship. His response surprised me to say the least, "What's got to be, gots to be." He finished his drink, threw a couple bucks on the counter and said, "Nice working with you, Bill." He walked out of the restaurant, and it was quite a while before I saw him again.

What we found out later was that during the fall of 1984, a guy by the name of Russell Buckner, also a convicted murderer, began transporting kilogram quantities of drugs to Brill and hundreds of thousands of dollars in cash back to Chicago.

Between the fall of 1984 and May of 1985 Buckner delivered 50 kilos or more of cocaine to Brill and about a million dollars to Diaz from Chicago. Buckner was also in the Wisconsin prison system for second degree murder charges and armed robbery charges. He killed a guy in a bar during an armed robbery. He met Brill in the state prison.

During the fall of 1984 and continuing until January of 1985, Randall Fisher, aka 'Fishman,' sold cocaine to an undercover Wisconsin Department of Justice agent. During January of 1985 on the third sale, Fisher was arrested. Fisher later provided information indicating that he had purchased cocaine from William Van Daal Wyk (Brill's go-to guy) on at least 10 occasions. Just like the other conspiracy cases, this one began to take shape. It was a good 14 or 16 months before we had a handle on exactly who was in the organization, what their role was, and how legally culpable they were.

During May of 1985, the team received information that Russel Buckner would be in possession of a quarter pound of cocaine. Acting on that information he was arrested, and the quarter pound of cocaine was seized. Based on information developed during the Buckner arrest, I screamed down to Milwaukee and obtained a search warrant for Brill's residence back in the Fox Valley. Prior to returning to the Valley, a search team had been assembled from the various agencies working the case. The minute I arrived at the search location; the warrant was executed.

Brill was cooperative during the execution of the search warrant and let us search with no resistance. Found during the search was $33,000 in cash but we couldn't find any drugs. As the search team was leaving his house, I noticed the closet door adjacent to the entrance of the home and had to wonder if that

closet had been thoroughly searched due to our hasty entrance. As we all gathered at the entry door ready to leave, I opened the closet door and noticed a cylindrical container which should have contained three tennis balls.

Having conducted dozens of search warrants with the Milwaukee Police Department's Vice Squad and having witnessed the discovery of cocaine in similar types of containers, got my attention. At almost exactly the same time the guys started leaving Brill's house was when I retrieved the tennis ball container and took the top off.

I was surprised, but not shocked, that the container was full of cocaine. Because we hadn't planned on ending the case at that point, I just seized the cocaine and the $33,000 and left as quickly as we entered. Brill must have been wondering why he wasn't arrested for possession of cocaine, but the plans to end the investigation needed to be finalized and fine-tuned.

During September of 1985 with all of our ducks lined up, we presented our case to the grand jury who returned a 32-count indictment charging Brill and five of his co-conspirators with various drug and tax counts. Independently, Brill was charged in 24 of the counts, the most serious being the Continuing Criminal Enterprise count which carried a sentence of 10 years to life.

The indictment charged that Brill managed an organization responsible for selling two and a half million dollars' worth of cocaine over a period of about 2 1/2 years. Simultaneous with the indictment, I obtained a federal search warrant for Brill's residence, which now was located in a different area of Northern Wisconsin. Brill moved after the May search warrant.

Prior to executing the search warrant, we assembled a team of agents and officers to execute it. When the time came to execute the warrant, I found Brill in the shower and arrested him

without incident. There was a safe in the house. I believed that we had to obtain an additional search warrant to break into it. Several hours later we opened the safe that contained $144,000 in cash that was seized along with a small amount of cocaine.

23

The Case Takes A Turn

Brill and several other co-defendants named in the indictment were held at the Waukesha County Jail until the detention hearing which occurred in early October. Prior to the detention hearing, a prominent Milwaukee attorney contacted me and told me that his client, Buckner, had information which was not only important to the case but important to the safety of people involved in the case. I knew there must have been something important cooking because this attorney, although very cordial, was a no-nonsense attorney who had never worked with DEA before.

At the appointed time, I met the attorney and his client in the Milwaukee office of DEA. Even I was surprised at the information I was about to receive. The client indicated that while he was incarcerated with Brill, as a result of the September arrest, Brill asked him for a couple of favors.

The first favor on the agenda was for Russell Bucker, to kill the main assistant United States attorney working on Brill's case. I was deeply troubled by this information, but there was more coming. Brill also asked Buckner to kill one of the primary witnesses in the case and was willing to pay $20,000 for each murder.

I didn't delay in relaying this information to the U.S. attorney's office in order to hold Brill accountable. The assistant United States attorney was a close personal friend of mine, and we had worked on many cases together. The AUSA was the first attorney to create a template which was used to qualify me as an expert witness. The AUSA and I had also tried several cases together, all successful. This would not be the last case we worked together!

Shortly after the disclosure of this information, a detention hearing was held for Brill in the U.S. magistrate's courtroom overseeing this case. I testified to the information about the two contract murders which raised the eyebrows of everybody in the courtroom including the magistrate. Needless to say, at the conclusion of my testimony, the Magistrate ordered that Brill remain in jail until his trial. The seriousness of the situation became apparent to Brill who, through his attorney, reached out with an offer to cooperate.

I am testifying at the detention hearing of Brill

I had a long-standing professional relationship with Brill's attorney, and we both respected each other's abilities and integrity. Brill's attorney was similar to the attorney who represented the witness who initially talked about the contract killings. The attorney was generally soft spoken, low keyed and very competent. He and I would always shake hands prior to a trial, but I quickly learned that the friendly handshake always gave way to a strong, well-prepared cross-examination. In other words I had to be prepared, or he would butcher me on the witness stand.

I had fond memories of participating in many trials with both of the attorneys related to the two hits, noting that at the end of every trial, the attorneys and I were always very cordial to each other and on occasions went out to a well-known Irish bar in town and had a cold one.

This time ironically, the two attorneys were on opposite sides of the court with me in the middle. I knew there was a lot of law enforcement who despised criminal defense attorneys, and I certainly could respect that. That notwithstanding, I still considered many of them friends and maintained those relationships to the present day.

After forging agreements with Brill's attorney, one of which was that the government would recommend 30 years in prison without parole, Brill agreed to cooperate with the government in an attempt to set up his Florida sources of supply, brothers Juan Restrepo and Armando Restrepo.

The mechanics of arranging a drug transaction when one of the parties was in jail was a little bit complicated but Brill worked it out. During this time, I got to spend some time with Brill and found him to be unemotional and cold, which was not unusual for a guy in his position. Brill was very similar to Dillard Kelley in attitude and demeanor.

I arranged to carry a special beeper and made arrangements for Brill to have access to a phone and tape recorder. To get the transaction going, the plan was for the Colombians in Miami to beep Brill, although I was actually carrying the beeper. After I would get a beep from Miami, I would contact the county jail that Brill was locked up in and have the deputies provide Brill with a phone and recorder to return the call and further the negotiations. Brill started negotiations with the Colombians in Miami at ten kilos of coke; however, the brothers were unable to come up with that amount and later Brill, at my direction, settled on seven kilos.

Eventually Carlos Restrepo flew to Milwaukee and hired a guy to drive a gray BMW containing seven kilos of cocaine from Florida to Milwaukee. After arriving in Milwaukee, Carlos checked into a hotel at the Milwaukee airport and at about 1a.m. a gray BMW showed up being driven by a Latin male in the company of a Latin female.

They also checked into adjoining rooms with Carlos. During this whole time, Milwaukee DEA was conducting a very tight surveillance on the airport hotel. Several hours later at about 2:30 in the morning Carlos, the female who accompanied him, and the driver of the BMW were arrested as they were leaving their hotel.

The BMW was seized and transported to the parking garage of the Federal Building, and Carlos and the driver of the BMW were placed in custody while the female was ultimately released. A search began of the BMW and literally resulted in us tearing it apart in an attempt to locate the 15 pounds of cocaine. Prior to completing the search, I reluctantly had to leave to meet a group of Milwaukee policemen.

Of course, after I left, the remaining agents discovered the cocaine hidden in a secret compartment in the car. At the time that was the biggest cocaine seizure in the state of Wisconsin's history. That seizure however essentially ended the active investigation into the James Brill organization, with the exception of unsuccessfully locating and arresting Armando Restrepo who probably fled to Colombia. Later, the case against Armando Restrepo was dismissed.

In the end, the investigation resulted in 11 arrests, the development of seven witnesses, the seizure of many cars, a 21-foot boat, interest in a business that was partially owned by Brill, $175,000 in cash and some stocks. Once again, the most important result of the above investigation was dismantling a large-scale cocaine organization operating in rural Wisconsin.

The cocaine organization was centered right in the middle of Nowhere, Wisconsin, but had far reaching tentacles. Not only was the local main source of supply arrested but his out-of-state sources of supply were also arrested, and one left the country and became a fugitive. All the arrests and search warrants executed during the above case were safe and nobody sustained any injuries.

All of the significant players in this conspiracy received prison sentences.

24

Too Close For Comfort

Considering all the arrests that I was involved in that required drawing my weapon (100% of the time), I was fortunate enough never to have to pull the trigger although I did come close on several occasions. The first occasion happened during 1976 when Augie and I had to arrest an informant who was caught selling cocaine on the side.

Augie and I agreed to meet him at a location close to downtown Milwaukee, and while Augie was talking to him on the phone to make arrangements to meet him, Augie could tell that he sounded very uneasy. His uneasiness coupled with a generally weird personality caused us both to be a little more cautious than we normally would when arresting an informant who had worked for us in the past. Both of us were well aware that this guy enjoyed snorting a line or two of cocaine.

We drove to the meeting place and saw his car backed against a building with him sitting in the front seat. As we approached his vehicle which was about 30 feet away, Augie started fanning out slightly to the left heading towards the passenger's door while I broke a little bit to the right and headed toward the driver's door. Although we were well acquainted with him, we were still cautious on the approach. Thankfully we didn't get too close as he pulled out what looked like a small caliber weapon and was pointing it alternately at Augie and me.

Augie and I drew our weapons and in a split second, both froze and aimed our weapons at the head of the now hostile informant. We naturally moved away from each other, causing the informant to have more difficult shots. We had three things going for us which we subconsciously recognized independent of each other.

First of all, we were about 30 feet from the informant which if he shot would have been a great shot from that distance with a small caliber weapon. Secondly, he had to shoot through a windshield which could have deflected the bullet's trajectory. Third and most important, neither Augie nor I thought the informant was capable of pulling the trigger.

Based on the above, both kept our aim square on the informant. "Drop your gun and get out of the car!" We simultaneously barked commands laced with profanity. "You will die if you don't!" After what seemed like forever but probably was only 30 seconds or so, the informant dropped the gun on the dashboard and raised both of his hands.

We cautiously approached him, sharpening our aims with each step forward. The closer we got to him, the more we realized he was high on some kind of drug with his glazed eyes and empty stare. I popped the front driver's door open, grabbed his left arm and threw him on the ground as hard and as fast as I could. Augie was right behind me, put a knee in the informant's back and cuffed him. His weapon turned out to be a little .22 caliber two shot Derringer.

Because the informant was arrested on probable cause, and we did not have a warrant, we took him to the DEA interrogation

room. After questioning him about the allegations that he was dealing cocaine, he of course did what all informants do. He offered to work for us and set up his cocaine source of supply for an arrest.

We chewed on the gun incident for quite a while and after conferring with our boss decided to kick him loose and have him shake the trees to see what fell. In today's world we wouldn't have the latitude of unilaterally deciding to turn our heads on both the gun and the cocaine violations, but it was what it was.

25

Another Close Call

The second incident occurred when I got a search warrant for a house on Milwaukee's far south side. According to the information the informant provided, the house had several Colombians staying there who possessed numerous weapons in the home along with kilos of cocaine. Because of the situation with the guns, I contacted the Milwaukee Police Tactical Unit, also known as the 700s.

They were called the 700s because their radio call sign always began with 700. (i.e. 701, 702, etc.) Not only were they the best in the business, but I had five or six members of the unit who were close personal friends, the bond only getting tighter on each dangerous entry they made on my behalf.

Ironically both DEA and the 700's were short staffed on the day the search warrant was going to be served. Upon assessing the manpower situation, the sergeant in charge of the tac unit told us that he would need me to join the entry team, being the last man through the door. I was told by several of the veteran 700 guys that they could not recall an instance where a non-tactical unit officer was allowed to accompany them on the breach.

The sergeant was one of two that I worked with over a period of 15 or more years. Both of them were as serious as a heart attack. This particular sergeant who looked like an army drill Sergeant, was 6 '2, muscular, with a gray crew cut and who was particularly serious. He demanded that his men practice safety to perfection. Frankly, I couldn't remember ever seeing him smile and didn't remember his name because everybody just called him Sarge. When things got bad and really went South in any of Milwaukee's many neighborhoods, it was the 700s who responded and put out the fire.

When bad-guy guns were involved in a search warrant, it was common practice that the time between the 'knock and announce' and the breach of the door was considerably shorter than when guns weren't involved. In fact, observing many doors being knocked down by the 700s, the common sequence followed was one or two loud knocks, followed by the announcement "Police," followed by a loud bang which meant the door had been breached.

Just how many seconds transpired between the initial knock and the door coming down would have to be left to individual interpretations. The only thing I knew for sure was that the 700s were the best tactical unit I ever worked with.

After the door was breached, I was probably the eighth or ninth guy in line and could hear a lot of commotion inside the house. The commands I was hearing by the tactical guys indicated that there were a lot more people in the house than anticipated. Somewhere in the middle of the loud commands, I heard a close friend on the tac squad, Jim Sanfilippo, call sign 702, holler out "Gun!" which was never good. What was good was that the exclamation wasn't followed by a gunshot.

☆ ☆

When I finally made it into the house, the living room on my right was full of tac guys on top of Colombians and everything seemed in order for the disorder that normally occurs during the initial moments of a search warrant. Prior to making entry, the sergeant told me that once I got into the house, I was to provide cover for his men. The sergeant protected his men as if they were his firstborn.

Unfortunately, or fortunately, just standing there waving my weapon at potential targets wasn't in my DNA. So contrary to the sergeant's orders, I walked toward the kitchen and found what I thought was a closet or pantry door that hadn't been cleared. All of the tac guys were occupied in the living room with a bunch of tired and unhappy Colombians most of whom were in a foul mood.

I quickly opened the door and to my surprise found a stairway leading to a darkened second floor. The informant did not tell us about the second floor so instinctively I hollered out "Attic!" flipped on the light switch and ran up the stairs. When I got to where I could see past the top step; I saw a bed with some stirring going on under the bed sheet. Within a second, I got a complete view of a bed five or six feet beyond the stairs. A Colombian was still lying down, awakening from a deep sleep.

Because he was still lying on his side, I saw his right arm on top of the sheets holding a big silver revolver. I skipped the traditional "Gun" announcement and screamed "Get your hands off the fuckin' gun!" several times. Although it seemed like a minute or two before he complied, it probably was only 15 or 20 seconds. He loosened his grip on the weapon, sat up and raised both hands in the air simultaneously.

I quickly approached him, shoved the gun off the bed, grabbed his arm and pulled him to the ground, jamming a knee

into his back before cuffing him. All in all, I thought I had done a pretty good job discovering a threat that until then we didn't know existed. Additionally, several more guns and a couple of kilos of cocaine were discovered during the subsequent search.

After the smoke settled, I was standing outside in the yard along with a couple other tac guys. Sarge left the house bearing the type of face that I could tell was not a happy face. He got right into my face and said, "If you ever do anything that stupid again, putting my men in jeopardy, you will never work with me or the tac squad again."

After Sarge returned to the house, I asked Squad 702, Sanfilippo, "What the heck did I do?"

Jim replied, "You said, Get your hands off the fucking gun" one too many times." The glint of a smile on the tac officer's face led me to believe that this wasn't the first time the sarge dressed somebody down.

I continued working with the "700s" for several more years, and although Sarge remained one of the supervisors, he never mentioned that incident again. To be frank, he didn't have to. Being in charge of a high-risk search warrant and having one of the participants acting independently of the team was a lesson well learned.

26
Mel

Sometime during the Bloomington, Indiana, deployment, I met an agent from the Indianapolis office by the name of Mel Schabilion. We immediately connected mostly because of our passion for fishing. Mel was a formidable presence. After the Bloomington deployment, he got transferred to Chicago, and we became close friends who ended up fishing at the Boundary Waters in Minnesota at least once a year and sometimes three or four times a year for a period of 20 years.

As I came to learn, Mel was a talented undercover agent, instructor, innovator and somewhat less than an adequate fisherman. Mel worked undercover and trained foreign police all over the world. He was also the first agent to be a dog handler and worked at O'Hare Airport for several years seizing millions of dollars in cash and piles of drugs thanks to the nose of his wonderful dog, Miss Katie. Mel also became one of DEA's best undercover agents. He was especially good when it came to clandestine labs. He taught himself how to process cocaine and was able to convince bad guys that he was in fact an expert in manufacturing cocaine hydrochloride.

Mel became part of my family, and he was the best man at Jeanne and my wedding. Throughout the whole time that I

knew Mel, whenever he called, wherever I was, he would tell whoever answered the phone that "The white prince of peace and happiness" was calling.

He and I also worked closely together on a number of cases even though he was assigned to the Chicago office while I was in the Milwaukee office. Mel was the perfect guy in case an undercover investigation required a strongman. One such investigation involved a member of a motorcycle gang from Lake County, Illinois. This case occurred sometime during the mid to early 1980s.

A deputy from Lake County, IL, who I had worked with on many cases contacted me and asked if I would like to work undercover on a motorcycle gang and that he had a very good informant who could introduce me to the gang guy. I immediately said yes, met and felt comfortable with the informant and was quickly introduced to Marty, a ranking member of the gang.

After I was introduced to Marty by the informant, we immediately felt comfortable with each other and started talking about Marty supplying me with some 'weight.' I made a couple small purchases, ounces, off of Marty in Lake County but then we started talking kilos of cocaine.

Marty was directed by his motorcycle gang to insist on doing a successful eight-ounce purchase before we started doing kilos. The Lake County Sheriff's Department provided me with plenty of information regarding the motorcycle gang, and an image quickly emerged indicating that they were not the type of guys anyone wanted at a family reunion.

Because of the violence associated with this gang, I reached out to Mel and asked him if he would be interested in acting as a heavy during the eight-ounce transaction which was going to turn into the arrest of Marty because I was stuck at the eight-

ounce level that DEA didn't want to buy. Mel readily agreed, received approval from the Chicago office, and I proceeded to handle the final details with Marty for the delivery to occur at a bar in Northern Lake County.

Arrangements were made for the final transaction, the time of the transaction, and the coordination of enforcement efforts with the Lake County Sheriff's Department who were supporting me. Mel and I drove to the bar, ordered a tap beer and waited for the arrival of Marty. The bar was dimly lit, and he had the distinct smell of stale beer. Mel and I were the only two customers in the bar which had seen better days. A surveillance team consisting of members from various agencies had already established surveillance locking in an area of about a mile from the bar.

While waiting, we periodically heard the roar of motorcycles driving past the bar and figured that we might be visited by more than Marty, so our senses were on high alert. Much to our surprise the motorcycle guys turned out to be just surveillance protecting Marty and no direct threat to us. The surveillance that was protecting Mel and I picked up on the counter surveillance being conducted by the motorcycle gang. It started looking a little dicey especially if the motorcycle gang tried to interfere with the arrest of Marty.

Finally at the appointed time, Marty entered the bar and stopped just short of me. I purposely didn't tell him that I was bringing a friend, especially a person the size of Mel which raised the normal level of paranoia Marty brought to the deal. When our eyes met, I kind of shrugged my shoulders, smiled and waved him over. Marty reluctantly came over and immediately asked who this monster of a man was that was sitting next to me.

I told Marty that Mel was my trusted partner and had half of the money for the cocaine. Because Mel had done hundreds

of undercover purchases, he developed a way of disarming drug dealers with his charm and a unique smile that conveyed both a warm feeling and at the same time a 'don't mess with this guy feeling.' Only people who worked undercover with him could really understand his complex smile.

That's exactly what Mel did when introduced to Marty. Marty immediately dropped his natural defenses and joined us at the bar for a drink. Regular drug deal talk occurred regarding whether I had the money and whether Marty had the dope. Marty stated that the cocaine was in a saddle bag in his motorcycle that was parked in the parking lot, and I told him that the money was in a car which was also in the parking lot. We slung back our beers and agreed to meet at Marty's motorcycle. Mel, Marty, and I set our beers down and walked out of the bar together. The motorcycle was parked about two spaces to the left at the exit of the bar. Our government car was parked about two spaces to the right of the exit of the bar.

As the two agents and one drug dealer approached the motorcycle, Marty walked to what would be the passenger side of the motorcycle, joined by Mel. I stood on the opposite side of the motorcycle facing Marty and Mel, who had discreetly slipped to a position behind and out of view of Marty. As Marty reached into the saddle bag, I saw Mel draw his .38 revolver and put it within inches of Marty's head from the back. Marty could either be reaching for a weapon or hopefully the drugs, but in either case it was game time. Marty couldn't see what Mel was doing. This was the time when the adrenaline started pumping knowing that in a matter of an instant, things could go south and lives could be changed if Marty was going to try to steal the money. Worse yet, if the motorcycle gang saw what was happening and

wanted to protect their cocaine, not knowing Mel and I were DEA, things could get really ugly. That thought did not escape either Mel or I, who were hypervigilant.

Fortunately, Marty withdrew a brown paper bag from the saddlebag and handed it over the motorcycle to me. I inspected the contents of the brown bag, which was a clear baggie full of white crystalline powder. The powder smelled like ether and upon close inspection had a pearlescent color strongly indicative of cocaine. I briefly looked at Mel. When our eyes met, with a nod of his head, Mel indicated that I should move a little to the right out of the line of fire. Simultaneously Mel told Marty, "DEA, put your hands up, step back, turn around and don't be stupid or your brains will be scattered in the parking lot."

As if rehearsed, I took a step or two back to the right, drew my weapon and pointed it at Marty yelling, "You heard the man!" Both Mel and I were very attentive to the sounds of motorcycles in case this was going to turn into a real shit show. Fortunately, the motorcycles had detected police surveillance and left Marty to fend for himself, the sounds of their motorcycles slowly fading in the distance. Fortunately, Marty immediately complied with the commands of the agents and was immediately handcuffed.

My deputy friend took custody of both Marty, the drugs and some non-drug evidence that we seized at the scene. Because neither Mel or I had any evidence to process or prisoners to process, we decided to get a cold drink and pat ourselves on the back for a safe and successful transaction.

My sister lived not too far from where the arrest occurred, so I called her up and told her to meet us at a bar both of us were familiar with in Wauconda, Illinois. When Mel and I arrived, my sister was already there and seemed to be in an exceptional mood which I should have seen as a red flag.

After closing time for the bar arrived, Mel and I returned to our respective residences and my sister to hers. As far as I knew, Mel and my sister had a nice evening and that was it. Several months later, I determined that Mel had other interests that I was previously unaware of. Without my knowledge, Mel started dating my sister ever since their first meeting and in fact had met my parents. This all came out during a conversation we were having, during which Mel mentioned my mother by a nickname only known to close family members, Mugsy.

I asked Mel, "How the heck do you know my mother's nickname?"

Being the typical seasoned undercover agent, he immediately threw it back at me and said, "You told me her nickname". Excellent move."

When two undercover guys knocked heads, the games they played with each other were amusing, which is what occurred over the next several weeks. Mel finally gave in and told me he had been dating my sister but only after I told him that I had talked to Mugsy, my mom's nickname, about Mel dating my sister. That of course wasn't true. I never talked to my mom about Mel and the sister!

As far as Marty's arrest went, he appeared before a judge, posted bond, was released, became a fugitive and died in Florida before he could be apprehended.

27

Mel, the Preacher, and I

While still assigned to Chicago my group supervisor assigned me to a senior agent who was nicknamed 'The Preacher.' Before he joined BNDD and then transitioned into DEA he was a real preacher. He soon joined the fishing trips that Mel and I started taking and loved so much. Preacher was a perfect fit, and we went up to the Boundary Waters in Minnesota for many years with The Preacher. On one occasion the three fishermen were scheduled to go to The Boundary Waters during August, but unfortunately The Preacher had corrective heart surgery performed in June.

Upon reflection, fishing wasn't the only reason we went up north. Mel, The Preacher, and I were extremely active agents involved in hundreds of undercover purchases and arrests. While fishing, we found solace in nature and the water of The Boundary Waters.

The transition from working undercover and making arrests to the simplicity of fishing provided a calm that was a needed replacement for the adrenaline-fueled world of drug law enforcement. It was also fun to pick on each other and vote who was the worst cook. Mel burned everything he put in the fry pan; The Preacher's specialty was rare northern pike with hard fried potatoes while my specialty was a combination of the above.

Catching a fish, cleaning it, and eating it then falling asleep under the stars provided us a chance to reconnect with a more authentic sense of who we were besides agents. It also provided us, our children and grandchildren with a common bond based on the simplicity of fishing.

We often swapped fishing stories, anecdotes and tales of our shared experiences which truly underscored the significance of our unspoken connection. The purpose of the stories provided entertainment for us, but more importantly provided insight into the psyche of three friends who were bonded by two passions, fishing and cops and robbers.

When we got to the base camp in the Boundary Waters, we still had a long way to travel to fish. We first took a four-mile boat ride. At the end of the boat ride was a portage that was four miles long connecting Moose Lake to Basswood Lake. In the middle of that four-mile portage was a pathway in the woods that connected to Ella Hall Lake.

Ella Hall Lake was where we fished when we only wanted to do a two-mile portage instead of the four miles to Basswood Lake. We never saw anybody else on the lake, so we had the lake all to ourselves every time we fished there. When Mel and I had extra money, we would pay a guy by the name of 'Jeep' to drive us the four miles from Moose Lake to Basswood Lake or to the shortcut to Ella Hall Lake. It was $20 for the long trip or $10 for the short trip to Ella Hall. For that fee we got to sit in the back of a 1940 something Jeep and drive over one of the roughest roads in North America.

The preacher told Mel that he wouldn't be able to go fishing because he was recuperating which would take at least eight weeks. Mel said that we were close enough to the eight-week recuperation time and insisted that The Preacher take the trip.

The Preacher finally agreed and up north we went. On the 12-hour ride to Ely, Minnesota, which is where we stopped for food, we both felt a little bit guilty due to The Preacher's restlessness and obvious pain that he was in. The guilt however didn't stop us from forging on and getting a line in the water.

After we got to the base camp, we started with the four-mile boat ride, followed by the two mile walk on a portage, followed by another half a mile walk through the path in the woods to our final destination, Ella Hall Lake. When there were waves on the lake, each one we hit reminded The Preacher of the scar he had on his chest.

Mel and I carried two canoes, a five and a half horse Evinrude motor, camping gear, bait, food, and fishing equipment all the way to Ella Hall Lake. The Preacher dragged his recuperating butt the whole way but didn't complain in true special agent form. Both Mel and I thought we were being extremely generous for not forcing The Preacher to carry anything too heavy.

What I didn't know was that during the walk to Ella Hall, Mel and The Preacher, scoundrels that they were, decided that I should be the one sleeping closest to the tent door. The reason for this was because bears were fairly common and routinely swam to islands like the one we camped on. When Mel and I were setting up camp, The Preacher suggested that we take a vote on who slept closest to the tent door.

I didn't realize it at the time, but this was the first of many pranks that were pulled during our fishing trips. The vote was two to one for ME to sleep at the door in the event that a bear came to visit our campsite. Just for the record my vote went to Mel because of his size. It made perfect sense to me.

When we finally arrived at the lake, Mel and I threw The Preacher in the back of one canoe with a large stone in the front

of his canoe to stabilize it. We tied a rope connecting his canoe to ours and paddled off to our favorite campsite. The Preacher was unable to paddle and had to be dragged around because of all the stitches from having his chest split open. The weather and the fishing were perfect, although it became somewhat tedious dragging The Preacher everywhere we wanted to fish.

We fished in different places because we didn't have much patience waiting for the fish to bite. The only kink in the fishing trip was when we were in a bay and The Preacher hooked into a huge northern pike which, because of his recent heart surgery, caused him significant pain trying to reel it in.

It was about this time when we started calling The Preacher 'Zippers' because when he took off his shirt to wash in the lake, his chest looked like it had a zipper running down it. We bathed in the lake and when they got thirsty dipped a tin cup straight in the lake and took a big drink. It was that clean!

There was no way in the world that he would be able to net the northern, so Mel and I unhooked the two canoes and paddled over to The Preacher who was grimacing in pain trying to get the fish close to the boat. The pain increased exponentially when every time he got the fish close to the boat, it took off on a run and put more pressure on his fairly new stitches. Finally, he got the fish close enough to the boat where Mel and I, who were doing somewhat of a balancing act in the canoe, were able to net it for him and bring it in our canoe. It weighed thirteen pounds which as the decades passed, the fish grew substantially to close to 20 pounds as the story was retold and embellish so many times.

The rest of the trip was mostly uneventful although I insisted that when we went fishing, the only food we brought was bread and lard to fry the fish in. The Preacher was quick to point out, after realizing that the only food they had was pure lard, that it was not on the food list recommended by his cardiologist. Mel suggested, with that half-crooked smile he had, that The Preacher boil his fish in lake water and enjoy the day. The preacher ate fish fried in lard!

28

Michigan Bikers

Sometime in the middle of my trips to Miami, I got another informant who told me about a couple of bikers from Michigan who would be willing to deliver kilogram quantities of cocaine to Milwaukee. The informant made plans over the telephone for these two guys to come to Milwaukee and negotiate with me and my Milwaukee partner, Augie. One day in February 1982, we met them at an airport motel by General Billy Mitchell Field and proceeded to negotiate kilogram prices for coke.

After we settled on a price, the two guys returned to Michigan after telling Augie and me they would talk to their source of supply and hopefully would be able to deliver several kilos to Milwaukee. After several phone calls between Augie and the Michigan guys, Augie said that we would first have to successfully purchase a half pound of cocaine and after that the door would be open for kilos. That was very typical and expected because good business sense almost dictated that the sellers of an illegal product would want to test the buyers with a smaller sample to make sure the buyers weren't police.

Augie and I agreed to meet the Michigan guys at the same hotel on a Saturday in early February 1982. At the appointed time Augie and I, being surveilled by the boss and one other

agent, entered the hotel and joined the two guys from Michigan who had arrived a little early. After exchanging greetings, they danced the typical dance. "Do you have the money?"

"Yeah, we got the money; you got the dope?"

Negotiations began and we settled on doing the transaction in a hotel room which Augie and I had previously rented. Augie and I, along with one of the guys from Michigan, Alan Springer, went up to the hotel room. After entering the hotel room, we told the dealer to show the dope and after we were satisfied with the quantity and quality, we would go to another hotel room and get the money. Obviously, this was just a line because there was no way in the world that we would be allowed to purchase a half pound of cocaine in the hopes of getting a couple kilos. So, the net result was that the Michigan bikers, if they had the coke, were going to jail.

Surprisingly, without much of a fuss, he agreed to show us the coke which he had tucked in the back of his pants. When Alan started reaching for the coke, both Augie and I tightened up a little bit thinking he may be going for a gun. He withdrew the coke and showed it to me. I smelled it and recognized the distinct smell of cocaine. Now it was just a matter of ending the charade of purchasing the coke and busting the guy.

Having worked undercover together on dozens of dozens of occasions, and without saying a word, Augie and I then both stood up, took a step or two back, drew our weapons, and told Alan he was under arrest. The hotel room was not the ideal place for an arrest, but we knew we had him and certainly if he did something stupid, the police would come out on top. What we didn't expect was that when we drew our weapons, he pulled a Schrade knife out of his back pocket, opened it and said it wasn't going to go down this way. Alan was shocked and pissed at the

same time and for a moment did not intend on having the deal end this way.

"I'm not taking the fall," he warned while waving the knife back and forth.

Augie answered with his commanding voice, "Drop the fucking knife!"

While he continued waving the knife and looking past us toward the door, I piped in, "Don't even think about it, drop it now!"

Augie, added, "I won't hesitate, fucker, lose the fuckin' knife!" Augie explained to him in a calm but forceful tone. If the dealer did anything stupid, it would be the last bad decision he made. A look of resignation appeared on the dealer's face, and he dropped the knife, knelt down as commanded and put his hands clasped over his head. I cuffed him while Augie kept his weapon pointed at center mass out of reach of the dealer but close enough for an easy kill shot if necessary.

I then called down to the restaurant and had my boss paged, advising him that our guy was under arrest and the coke seized. I also asked the boss and the other agent to arrest whoever was left in this deal. Our boss explained that there were two other guys, including a Latin male who turned out to be a Colombian, Eduardo Alfonseo, also sitting in the restaurant. We decided to go ahead and arrest them which occurred without incident. Ironically Alfonseo admitted in court that he had only been in the United States for a week and was on a one-month visa. It was a safe arrest, everybody complied, yet as it turned out, nobody cooperated.

When the three defendants appeared before a U.S. magistrate on Monday morning for a bond hearing, a very surprising revelation was revealed. The guy who pulled the knife during

the arrest, told the magistrate, through his attorney, that he had been a member of a motorcycle club in California.

He told the magistrate that he visited the infamous Charles Manson at the Spahn Ranch several days after the Tate/Labianca murders, during August 1969, in an attempt to find one of the motorcycle club members who was missing. The notoriety of murders and the gruesome nature of the crime generated worldwide headlines.

Springer continued telling the magistrate that when visiting the ranch, Charlie Manson told him that he had very recently killed five people, which was the total number of people murdered in the Tate/Labianca homicides. That information eventually ended up with the Los Angeles authorities who used it to develop a crucial witness in the case against Charles Manson and his Helter-Skelter followers. The guy with the knife testified at the Manson trial indicating that Manson had told him that 'the family' referring to Manson's cult followers, had just murdered 5 people. The disposition of the three arrestees is unknown.

29
More Michigan

Within months of the case detailed above, in the early to mid 1980s, I developed another informant who provided credible information about a businessman from Michigan who was interested in finding a new source of supply for pure cocaine. It didn't take long to call my buddy Mel in Chicago to see if he'd be interested in working undercover on this deal. As was typical, Mel responded, "Where and when, and I'll be there." Mel laid down a cover story with the informant. For this case, how many deals Mel and the informant had done, how long they knew each other, where they met, etc.

The informant contacted the businessman and laid down background information on his cocaine source of supply, Mel. The businessman jumped at the opportunity to meet Mel and purchase some very high-quality cocaine. After negotiations were conducted on the phone, an agreement was reached between the informant and the businessman. It became very clear during negotiations that the informant and the guy from Michigan were much more than casual acquaintances and had conducted drug deals in the past.

Plans were made for the Michigan businessman to come to Milwaukee to meet the guy who could produce cocaine. Once

again on a Saturday, strictly by coincidence, the Michigan guy flew into Milwaukee and checked into a hotel under the surveillance of Milwaukee DEA agents. After he checked into the hotel, he called the informant and told him to meet Mel in the businessman's hotel room.

At the appointed time, both Mel and the informant proceeded to the businessman's hotel room where introductions were conducted. Mel gave him the typical spiel relating to Mel's ability to convert cocaine base into cocaine hydrochloride and doing so in kilogram quantities. Mel told the guy that he had several kilograms located nearby if the guy had the appropriate amount of money for the transaction. Previously the businessman had agreed with the informant to bring enough money to buy two kilograms of pure cocaine.

After Mel was convinced that this guy was the real thing, the businessman was provided with a room number in the same hotel and a time to go to that room with the money. After Mel left, allegedly to get the cocaine and right before the appointed time for the meeting, surveillance watched as the businessman left his room and walked to a parking lot associated with the hotel and retrieved a good-sized briefcase from the trunk of what turned out to be a rented car.

Actions like this almost always meant that we were going to have a deal, but in an attempt to try to cover the informant, I decided to change the game plan a little bit. Another agent and I stationed ourselves around the corner from the room to which we anticipated the businessman was going to walk. We were in radio contact with another agent who observed that the businessman was walking to the appointed and agreed upon room.

As the businessman approached the room occupied by Mel, I walked around the corner with the other agent and both of us

displayed our badges and announced that we were police and had some questions for him. With no hesitation, the businessman gave the briefcase to my partner. Before we could even give him his Miranda warnings, he indicated that there was a lot of cash in the briefcase and that he wanted to cooperate.

The whole DEA team returned to the Milwaukee office where the money was counted, processed, (i.e. placing the money in a sealed plastic bag with the initials of two agents verifying the amount and witnessed the counting) and placed it in the office safe.

We felt that the businessman posed no harm to the informant, so we brought Mel into the debriefing being conducted. The businessman told Mel and me that he wanted to cooperate 100%. He also indicated that he could set up several individuals in Michigan and would be willing to testify against them.

After both Mel and I were convinced that the businessman was sincere, we gathered as much information as we could from him, gave him a receipt for the money, and told him to have a Michigan agent call first thing Monday morning. This was to ensure that the businessman was following through with his promise to cooperate. After that we patted him on the ass and sent him on his way. As predicted, the first thing Monday morning I received a call from an agent in Michigan who told me that he had been contacted by the informant and they were very happy with the information provided.

Later I learned that the informant made several significant cases for the Michigan offices and based on the quality of the cases, the agents in Michigan recommended that the businessman not be charged. I talked to Mel about the proposal, and both agreed that the informant needed to produce one more case for Michigan and that charges would not be pursued. I called Michigan and relayed the information and believe it or not within a week we were able to squeeze one more case out of the businessman. Another case was closed on our end. Time to move on.

For the above surveillance, The Chicago office sent a rookie up to help. He was privy to everything including what happened once we returned to the Milwaukee office. This may have been the biggest case he had seen in his short career, and he had a blank stare in his eyes when we escorted the bad guy out of the office and told him to have a Michigan agent call Monday morning. Before leaving the office, he asked, "Are you done with me?"

I answered, "Yeah, thanks for your help."

He looked at me like there has got to be more to the story, but there wasn't.

30

You Meet People
In the Strangest Places

As is well documented, cocaine trafficking exploded in the United States in the late '70s and continued into the 80s. Because Miami was the source city of cocaine for both Milwaukee and Chicago, Mel and I had to make frequent trips to Miami in either an undercover capacity or in an investigative capacity. Our trips were so frequent that we purposely scheduled Miami or Fort Lauderdale trips to coincide with each other so that we could either go to jai alai or have a good steak at Chuck's in Fort Lauderdale.

During about early of 1984, before we started actually scheduling our trips to coincide with each other, I arranged to meet two Colombians at a hotel and negotiate a multi-kilo cocaine transaction. When I called the Miami support group to coordinate my trip, I was told they were extremely busy and would not be able to provide surveillance, but to call them if I needed anything. Because no money or drugs were involved, I was allowed to go on the trip. During that time period there was no doubt in my mind that they were truly busy and couldn't spare any extra men to cover the meeting with the Colombians.

☆ ☆

So, I flew down to Miami and walked into the hotel lounge at the appointed time to meet the Colombians. The first guy I saw sitting at the bar was a crime reporter from the largest newspaper in Chicago. I had previously befriended him during the Carbondale deployment which he was covering as a feature crime story.

I kept in touch with him and both of us were taken aback when our eyes met as soon as I entered the bar. Being a long-time crime reporter and knowing what was going on in Miami, John waited for me to first acknowledge him. I gave him a brief smile enough to confirm the recognition but not enough to be friendly and continued walking past him. John returned the smile and quickly turned his head as I kept on walking past the reporter. Unfortunately, we haven't spoken since, but he knew I was in the middle of something.

I walked farther into the bar and saw two guys that fit the description of the Colombians that I was supposed to meet. I ordered a drink after which negotiations commenced just like all drug negotiations. In the middle of negotiations and after about three beers, I went to the men's room. While at the urinal, my peripheral vision allowed me to see a large man walk to the urinal next to me. Without even looking at me, the man said, "Hey, Willy, what are you doing in Miami?"

I immediately recognized the voice, and trying to mask the fact that I was a little startled, didn't turn my head but responded, "What does it look like I'm doing?"

Mel replied, "Dumbbell."

I asked Mel, "What are you doing in Miami?"

Mel replied, "I'm doing the same thing that you're doing."

Although neither Mel nor I indicated we were trying to do a drug deal, we both instinctively knew that the only reason for being in a Miami men's room at an airport hotel room was a drug deal.

We both said "Cool" and then Mel asked if I wanted to meet him and his partner Harry at Jai Alai after the negotiations. As I was leaving the restroom, I asked Mel if Mel had seen John, the Chicago crime reporter. Mel replied that he had but didn't want to talk to him for obvious reasons. Later that night I met both Mel and Harry at Jai Alai and lost a few bucks.

Negotiations with the Colombians dragged on persistently and after an extended effort, I found himself back in Miami. Frustrated with the Colombians insistence on delivering a sample before a much larger load, I managed to have a two-kilo sample delivered to the same hotel where I met Mel. Unfortunately, the Colombians held firm, and the case hit a dead end after the uneventful delivery of two kilos of cocaine in Miami. Three Colombians were arrested and presumably got insignificant jail time because they were in Miami.

Shortly thereafter in an unrelated conversation, Mel casually inquired about the outcome of my meeting with the Colombians. I explained that I secured a two-kilo sample, but the Colombians remained uncooperative, bringing the investigation to a standstill.

Curious about Mel's endeavors, I asked Mel if he had any success with his contacts. For background, Mel had established an undercover chemical company, selling substances crucial for illegal drug production. The operation involved tracking the chemicals to uncover illicit drug laboratories and orchestrating busts at the opportune moment throughout the United States and sometimes around the world.

Mel revealed that he had sold a very large quantity of ether, a key component in cocaine production, to the Colombians he

met in Miami. Mel continued stating that a surveillance team traced the chemicals to the port of New Orleans and then to Colombia. The result was a successful operation, leading to the arrest of numerous individuals, the seizure of multiple labs, and the confiscation of a significant amount of cocaine and precursor chemicals. I was impressed with the above information and congratulated Mel.

As our conversation drifted into casual banter, little did I know that Mel's operation would soon make world headlines. A news report and a DEA enforcement teletype informed me that a clandestine cocaine lab in Tranquilandia, Colombia, had been busted. The operation yielded 14 clandestine cocaine labs, seven airplanes, over 10,000 pounds of precursor chemicals, and a staggering 30,000 pounds of cocaine.

Connecting the dots, I suspected this was the same operation Mel had mentioned earlier. Eager to confirm, I called Mel and asked if he played a role in the Tranquilandia cocaine laboratory's takedown. With his trademark straightforwardness, Mel confirmed, "Yeah, dumbbell, those were the guys I sold the ether to that I met in Miami." (Mel used the word dumbbell as a term of endearment)

I made many more trips to South Florida, unfortunately too many to remember, but I did recall the results of two specific trips. Each of these involved multi-kilograms of cocaine and the arrest of multiple defendants. Fortunately, one of the individuals arrested during the cocaine delivery provided information linking a high-level government official from Bermuda with drug trafficking. A Miami or Fort Lauderdale agent that I had been working with gave me a phone call and told me about the arrest of the official in Bermuda.

In the second case, the guys I arrested, according to Miami special agents, were suspected of taking some of their competitors on a deep-sea fishing trip. The competitors never returned to shore, and it was believed that they were murdered at sea and fed to the sharks. The fellows that ended up being shark food were unwitting rivals of the seemingly generous fishing guides who were eliminating competition in the cocaine business. During the mid-1980s incidents like this happened all the time either in the ocean or in the Everglades. I never did follow up on the adjudication of any of the Miami cases nor was I ever required to go to court, so I assume they all pled guilty

31
One More Fishing Trip

A couple years later Mel, The Preacher, and I repeated our annual fishing trip even going to the same lake. This time all three special agents hauled in all of our equipment and put a 16-foot Lund boat and motor on a set of wheels that we used to push the two miles necessary to get to Ella Hall Lake. Then we had to push the boat down the same narrow path we traversed several years earlier to the lake. We set up camp at a different campsite and enjoyed catching smallmouth bass and northern pike during the next several days.

One late afternoon The Preacher (aka The Zipper) was cleaning some fish on the shoreline. At this particular moment he happened to be cleaning a pretty good-sized northern pike with a Rapala fishing knife. Having no sense of humor about being fileted, the fish flopped around and drove the Rapala knife right through the Preacher's arm causing him to immediately react with a train of vulgarity. After fortunately determining that nothing vital had been severed, like in the movies, we decided to remove the knife and cover it with the only thing we had available, which was an old, unsanitary towel that we used to dry the fish before cleaning. We did rinse the towel out in the lake before using it as a wrap.

Preacher was able to move all of his fingers and really wasn't bleeding that badly. Although the end of the knife did not penetrate all the way through his arm, a nice little bump appeared on the opposite side of the puncture wound. We proceeded to cover the wound tourniquet style and decided that Preacher needed professional medical care as opposed to Mel's and my Ella Hall Lake emergency room.

After the bleeding had stopped, Mel and I helped Preacher through the wooded pathway to the portage, which was 1/2 mile long, knowing that at 5 p.m. one of the guides would be coming past the rudimentary path to the lake where we were fishing. During those times the only people that we'd see when fishing in the back country would be those we were fishing with and an occasional guide.

The Preacher agreed to the plan that Mel and I devised. Part of the plan was to pin a note on him explaining the situation and asking the guide to drop him off at the entrance to the same path as soon as he had seen professional medical people. The first night Mel and I walked out to the portage at 5:00 and the friendly guide told us that The Preacher was still in Ely recovering.

The second night at 5 p.m. we again walked the pathway to the Portage and low and behold The Preacher was leaning against the same tree where we had dropped him off two nights' prior. He also had a bag full of goodies to eat because Mel and I still stuck to the lard and bread regimen. Sometime during this trip, The Preacher's nickname changed to the 'Old Ranger.'

The change only occurred because when he tied his fishing line, he had to use a pair of reading glasses. By now his chest zipper had healed. It took about 15 minutes and during this eternity the Old Ranger was holding the line and hook and squinting as if he was looking at a solar eclipse. During this

excruciating time period, Mel and I would be mimicking his squinting and fumbling around until all three of us were belly laughing. We enjoyed that great therapy! Of course, it wasn't too much longer that Mel and I were both using reading glasses for just about everything.

On several of the trips to The Boundary Waters, our sons accompanied us and on one occasion my daughter accompanied us. Our children remained friends and kept in touch with each other. It has been very gratifying for me to see the kids grow up and share Boundary Water tales just as Mel and I did. Mel's son and grandson recently took a trip up to the Boundary Waters with a Boy Scout Troop. Coincidentally, Mel's son and daughter-in-law both spent 20 plus years in federal law enforcement.

32

Skag, Horse, Junk, Smel, H, White, Black Tar, Chiva, Boy, Brown

No matter what you call it, it's still heroin. I called it the dirty drug and hated it with great passion for what it did to people. I witnessed firsthand the devastating effect heroin had on people and carry some of those memories with me to this day. One particular event that happened remained a stark reminder of the pain and suffering caused by heroin.

While in a small city in Southern Illinois, an informant brought me to a house with the intention of getting one of the occupants to sell me some heroin. Being very early in my career, the informant was not debriefed sufficiently and forgot to tell me that there was a party going on there involving mostly heroin users, dealers and dealer/users.

The one thing about heroin users is that they will do anything to anybody for a fix if they need it. They usually have brown circles under their eyes, are thin and wear long sleeve shirts, even if it's 90° out. The shirts are to hide the lines left on their

forearms when they inject the heroin. I entered the house and was surprised to see 10 or 15 people mingling around.

The informant made a general introduction of me to the gathering of people. This informant must have been trusted by the people at the house because everybody seemed okay with bringing a stranger into the house. The fact of the matter was that I later found out that most of the people were high and didn't really care about strangers at that point.

I sat down on a couch occupied by one other guy at the other end who was whispering something to a girl and between sentences was staring at me. I tried to remain calm and collected which apparently worked because the girl left and returned shortly with a 12-inch rubber lace, water, some heroin on the plate, a teaspoon, lighter and a syringe. All the fixings for a great high.

Trying not to pay attention to what was going on three feet away, I then saw the girl inject the guy with the heroin in the big vein on the inside of the arm above the elbow. I turned my head for a second trying to be disinterested, and when I turned my head back in the direction of the guy who just got the shot of heroin, I saw the guy's head leaning back on the couch, mouth wide open seemingly unconscious.

In that nobody else was particularly concerned, I remained nonchalant. The thought ran through my head that this guy may have just overdosed and could be on the way to the spirit in the sky. I also realized that if I acted like a policeman and tried to save this guy, I very well could join him and the spirit in the sky.

I do not remember if I was successful in purchasing any heroin on that evening, but I do remember the guy with his head leaning on the back of the couch with his mouth wide open and spit running down his cheek. What was happening in layman's

terms was the guy was 'nodding' because of the effects of heroin. I had a sour taste about heroin dealers and the poison they sold after that experience. Although it was difficult to purchase heroin, not looking like a junkie, I pursued every opportunity I had to remove heroin dealers from the streets.

33

A Little More Heroin

After the arrests in the case of the mini bennies that was part of CENTAC-4 which involved the small white pills called white crosses back in 1974, one of the arrested guys became a long-time DEA informant and worked for several offices throughout the country. It just happened that in August of 1982 the informant bumped into a Milwaukee guy, Mario Fragosa, and they got to talking. The meeting occurred in Los Angeles. Fragosa told the informant that he was from Milwaukee and was a heroin dealer.

The informant told Fragosa that he was familiar with Milwaukee only because he was arrested there and in fact knew a guy who lived in Milwaukee that was also quite the dealer. The informant put Fragosa and me together on the phone, and after several conversations, it was decided that Fragosa would bring a one-ounce sample of heroin back to Milwaukee to sell to me for $2,100. As the evidence later showed, Fragosa obtained 2.5 grams of pure heroin from Juan Garcia in Los Angeles. (28 Grams equals one ounce so 2.5 g is less than a tenth of an ounce for $2,100 to put it in perspective) Fragosa then flew back to Milwaukee anticipating selling one ounce of heroin.

With the cooperation of the Los Angeles DEA office, both Fragosa and his source for heroin, Juan Garcia were identified,

so I knew exactly who he was dealing with. Fragosa was well known to law enforcement in Milwaukee and his reputation was not good. When Fragosa returned to Milwaukee, he mixed the 2 1/2 grams of pure heroin with 25 ½ grams of an adulterant. (An adulterant is a water-soluble substance commonly used to increase the bulk of heroin, dilute its purity and increase the dealer's profit.) If somebody would have injected the two and a half grams of pure heroin, they would have been dead in minutes.

After cutting the heroin, he contacted me and took steps to meet at a Milwaukee airport hotel to complete the sale. The informant did an excellent job of selling me to Fragosa because there was none of the paranoia normally exhibited during the first drug sale that occurred between two people. In addition, I still had long hair and a beard with a brown floppy hat which helped put Fragosa at ease. I did not look like a cop.

During a conversation before the transaction, I indicated that I would purchase a kilo of heroin if the one-ounce sample was as good as Fragosa said it would be. Fragosa told me without hesitation that he could obtain a kilo of heroin within a couple of days and deliver it at the same hotel in Milwaukee. Fragosa further indicated that if the kilo went well, he could turn around and obtain three kilograms again to deliver in Milwaukee. An agreement was reached and Fragosa gave me one ounce of heroin, and I gave Fragosa $2,100 in return.

I returned to the Milwaukee DEA office and field tested a very small sample of the ounce of heroin and received a positive reaction for the presence of heroin. This was all that was needed for me to place a call to Fragosa to order the kilogram of cocaine. A price was agreed upon.

In the meantime, Fragosa jumped on the first transportation headed west after making arrangements with Garcia to purchase

four ounces of pure heroin for $8,000 an ounce. Fragosa met with Garcia, the heroin source of supply, in Los Angeles and received the four ounces of heroin on consignment and jumped on the first plane heading east.

After Fragosa arrived in Milwaukee, he rented a hotel room and called me to set a time to meet for the transaction. Before the meeting, Fragosa had to add 36 oz of an adulterant to the four ounces of pure heroin so it equaled one kilo, or 1000 grams, 2.2 lbs. After preparing the kilogram, he had to properly package it. Basically, he was placing the heroin in a plastic bag forming a brick and then wrapping it and securing it with duct tape.

At the same time Fragosa was cutting the heroin, I was withdrawing $50,000 from the DEA office to use for the alleged purchase which in fact was going to be an arrest after I saw the heroin. Surveillance plans were made and I drove to the hotel and walked to the room where Fragosa said he would be. With a couple of beads of sweat on my forehead, I knocked on the door and was admitted to the room by Fragosa, who also had a few beads of sweat on his forehead.

After a brief discussion, I told Fragosa that the money was in a car in the parking lot of the hotel, but I wanted to see the heroin before transferring the money. Fragosa retrieved the brick shaped package wrapped in duct tape from under his bed with little hesitation. There was no doubt in my mind that the informant had done an excellent job in selling me as a future prospect because at this point all Fragosa was seeing was a lot of $100 bills. The heroin was placed under the bed as Fragosa and I walked to the car where the money was secured.

I showed Fragosa the money that was to be used for the alleged purchase, secured it in the trunk of the OGV, which was under very close surveillance, and both Fragosa and I returned

to the bar to have a celebratory drink before consummating the deal. While in the bar I gave a pre-arranged arrest signal to a couple of surveillance agents who were also in the bar and Fragosa was quickly and quietly arrested without incident. The kilo of heroin was seized from the hotel room, and the money was returned to the DEA office along with the prisoner.

It didn't take long for Fragosa to see the light, and he began cooperating. I had him place several recorded phone calls to Garcia in Los Angeles. The primary purpose of the phone calls was to have Garcia admit that the heroin sold to me, in fact, came from Garcia.

That was not much of a problem because Garcia wanted the $8,000 for the four ounces of heroin that he had given to Fragosa on consignment in Los Angeles a day or so earlier. During the phone calls, Garcia was focused only on the $8,000 that Fragosa offered him for the four ounces and insisted that Fragosa come to Los Angeles and pay Garcia! After I got my admissions from Garcia with the recorded calls, an arrest warrant was issued for Garcia, and he was arrested in Los Angeles sometime during September.

Both Garcia and Fragosa were convicted and sentenced to federal prison. Fragosa ended up testifying against Garcia and with the testimony and telephone tapes, Garcia was easily convicted.

34

Heroin Backstory

Not long after I was on the job, I had contact with several people addicted to heroin and found there was a different tragic story to each of them. The story that stood out the most and affected me the most was about a Mexican migrant farmer who worked the fields in southeastern Wisconsin. Sisto had a wife and six children and a lifelong addiction to heroin. I arrested him after he sold a small quantity of heroin to me. Despite his addiction, he was a likable guy, and I immediately realized the strength of a heroin addiction over a person's life.

After working with Sisto, I got a call one day with a request to meet him on the farm. He told me that if anybody was around, for me to pretend that I was just a friend. I went to the farm with another agent and met with Sisto who was with his wife and six children. After introducing me to his family, he asked if we could have a private conversation which, based on his family's reaction, was not unusual for him.

When alone with me and the other agent, Sisto, who was a large man, pathetically asked if there was anything DEA could do to help with his addiction. Having never been confronted with a situation like this, as gently as possible I said the DEA was not a rehabilitation agency. Sisto went on to tell a story how Mexican

heroin addicts would grab a couple bottles of Jack Daniels, a couple of friends, and lock themselves in a house until they were done with withdrawals.

The request sounded easy enough, and I was all in. I got permission from my boss to take Sisto to a hotel in Port Washington, Wisconsin, and spend two days for a complete debriefing of Sisto regarding heroin trafficking in southern Wisconsin. I got the money for the hotel and meals and met Sisto in Port Washington.

Of course, there were two bottles of Jack Daniels transported by the government car for the 'intense debriefing.' Ironically, the other agent on this mission loved Jack Daniels and was happy to assist. Starting several hours after we got there and continuing well into the next day was a barrage of sweating, throwing up, a racing pulse, and diarrhea.

On several occasions I thought Sisto was about to die, but each time I tried to call for an ambulance, Sisto talked me out of it. After two very stressful days, Sisto indicated that the worst was over and to get him home to his family. Although the withdrawal symptoms continued, Sisto could now look at his family and say he tried. And try he did. The last time I ever saw him was when he got in his car and started driving home. He did place a brief telephone call to me several months later and simply said "Thanks."

To see a proud man reduced to something that was very difficult to describe, indeed left a lifelong impression on me. I believe that anybody who has sympathy for heroin dealers and provide lame excuses for their behavior belong in the same cell as dealers.

35

Reverse Undercover Deal

During the early part of 1985 Harry got a call from a prominent cocaine dealer who had connections throughout the country. This call came only after Harry and his IRS colleagues developed a strong tax case against the potential informant. During this call it was determined that the cocaine dealer wanted to become an informant. This particular fellow was probably one of the first guys to smuggle cocaine directly from Columbia to Chicago.

As he described it, in the early days of cocaine smuggling all he had to do was look confident in business attire when going through either Colombian or U.S. Customs. His arrogance which developed over the years was probably what made him a successful smuggler.

Much of the information that he provided was new to IRS Agent Harry, but a quick check of DEA's computer system verified all of the information the informant was providing. Because the information was about dealers located in the Chicago area, I placed a call to Good Old Reliable Mel and asked if he would be interested. Never one to turn down a good drug deal, Mel said he was all in and if necessary, he could get as much help as necessary from Chicago DEA people.

Harry and I reached an agreement with the informant where he would get a percentage off all proceeds seized during reverse undercover operations, and that we would not reveal his identity as an informant. This was pretty standard during those hectic times when cocaine was flooding into the United States.

He was very bright, arrogant and loved money, so for the most part he became an excellent informant who we nicknamed 'Point Man.' After finalizing our agreement, Harry and I sent Point Man on his way to locate known drug traffickers and let them know he had a good connection for high quality reasonably priced cocaine.

One of the first dealers the informant could set up was a guy by the name of Gil Hitchens who was a well-known cocaine trafficker in the Chicago suburban area. After presenting Hitchens with the possibility of selling him cocaine, arrangements were made with the Point Man, Hitchens, and Mel to meet at a Chicago Rush Street Bar and initiate negotiations to see how much cocaine Hitchens could afford.

This strategy was known as a reverse undercover operation because the government would allegedly be selling the cocaine to the drug dealer. I asked the bosses to use Mel as the undercover agent because he was from Chicago, knew the lay of the land, and could sell sand to the Arabs.

Normally when conducting reverse undercover operations, extreme care had to be taken to prevent rip-offs which could escalate into violence. Hitchens's reputation was that of a good honest cocaine dealer, and Mel and I weren't too concerned about violence, although our antennas as usual were always up.

On the given day, Hitchens, the Point Man and Mel met at the restaurant. Mel charmed Hitchens with his credentials as a cocaine chemist who could provide the highest quality product.

Hitchens jumped on the chance of purchasing cocaine from Mel and placed an initial order of 10 kilos at $43,000 a kilo. As in any cocaine transaction, Hitchens asked for a sample which Mel was ready for.

At that time, for a DEA agent to provide any type of drug to a trafficker, hoops had to be jumped through and all kinds of layers of authority had to approve the transfer up to the administrator of DEA and the attorney general. All the i's had been dotted and t's had been crossed so Mel, Hitchens, and the Point Man left the restaurant and entered Mel's vehicle where Mel provided Hitchens with one gram of pure cocaine.

Hitchens had previously told Mel that he would be able to analyze the sample and verify that it was in fact pure. That being the case, Hitchens indicated his next order would be for 35 kilos of cocaine. Arrangements were made for the Point Man and Mel to meet Hitchens at a Lombard Hotel during the spring of 1985. Prior to the meeting, surveillance agents got together and formulated an airtight plan to protect Mel during the transaction. All exits were covered as well as a couple of hotel rooms located close to the one that Mel and the Point Man would occupy.

Mel and Point Man arrived at the agreed time and checked into their room. Finally, Hitchens arrived carrying two attaché bags. Concealed in each of the attaché bags was $215,000 in $100 bills. Hitchens apologized to Mel for being a little bit late. Mel had no problem lecturing Hitchens about the importance of being prompt during transactions. The longer a drug deal takes, the greater the chances of getting busted. Mel told Hitchens in no uncertain terms that nobody was going to get busted today because Hitchens had to finish a joint before the drug deal.

Mel opened the attaché cases and fanned the money to make sure there was no blank paper or anything else deceptive as in

a Philadelphia Flash. (A Philadelphia flash is a stack of money with the top and bottom bills being hundreds and everything in the middle being paper cut the same size as a $100 bill) Mel counted one stack of hundreds and made a quick estimate that all the money was there. That was more for show than anything else, Mel pretending to be a big dealer.

Unfortunately, Mel didn't wear a recorder during his meeting in the hotel room for the same reason no agents liked wearing a recorder. That reason was very simple: If he was patted down and a recorder was located, there would be big problems with no good solutions.

Mel, Point Man, and Hitchens left the hotel room. Previously all agents assigned to the surveillance were made aware of the fact that when Hitchens and Mel got to the lobby of the hotel, and they stayed together, the arrest of Hitchens could be made. If they had parted ways, that meant there was no deal and for surveillance not to take any action. Because surveillance had already seen Hitchens arrive with two attaché cases, the surveillance team was more than ready to take action.

When the elevator doors opened, Hitchens, Mel, and Point Man began walking toward the exit of the hotel which led directly to the parking lot. Because they stayed together all the way to the hotel exit, it was bust time. Based on prior experience, gut feelings and surveillance observations, Harry and I decided on conducting the arrest as quietly as possible. We approached Hitchens and the others and identified ourselves, and we asked them what their business was.

At this time Hitchens, who was carrying the attaché bags, set them down and Harry asked who the owner of the attaché bags was. Both Hitchens and Mel denied owning the suitcase, and Point Man remained silent. At that moment Harry said that

he was the new owner of the attaché bags, adding that he had just stopped at the hotel for a few cocktails and was surprised at the inadvertent meeting at the hotel. I could tell at this point that Mel was anxious, so we prearranged to separate all three of the prisoners for questioning.

When I got Mel alone, Mel simply wanted to move things along so we could process the prisoner and the cash and have a cold drink. Even though Mel had quit drinking several years earlier, he still enjoyed going to bars with the boys after a decent bust. So, we hurried things along and processed Hitchens, made an official count of the money, and secured it in a DEA safe.

Three agents participated in counting the cash and after three consecutive counts, came up with $430,000. The money was secured, and everybody involved in the case except for Hitchens went to a German restaurant/bar which was located right next door to the federal building in Chicago. Of course, Point Man was dismissed and not invited to the bar.

A couple of months after the sting, DEA headquarters approved a $50,000 reward for Point Man. Not long after the approval, Mel and I met Point Man in a junkyard. Holding up DEA's end of the bargain, I paid Point Man and thanked him for his services indicating that we would certainly work with him again if something came up. The reason more than 10% of the reverse undercover proceeds was given to Point Man was because he had worked for DEA over a period of several years and deserved an enticement to keep on working.

36

Texas Dealers

During the summer of 1983, information was received by the Wisconsin Department of Justice that a couple of Colombians were located in Texas who were looking for a new outlet of cocaine. Because I was working closely with them at the time, they contacted me and asked if I would be willing to do the undercover work. After record checks, I contacted the agent at the Wisconsin Department of Justice and told him I would be happy to help.

An informant provided by state justice contracted for the Colombians to come to Milwaukee to meet me with a one-kilo sample of cocaine. The date for the transaction was set. The Colombians contacted me to meet at a restaurant in Milwaukee.

Surveillance plans were coordinated between the Milwaukee DEA and the State Justice Department. I placed $64,000 in the trunk of an official government vehicle and proceeded to the restaurant while being surveilled by Milwaukee DEA agents. As is usual, the Colombians were late for the meeting and just as I was getting ready to call off the deal, two of the Colombian showed up

Prior to beginning negotiations, one of the Columbians asked me to stand up after which he performed a quick pat down looking for a gun. He clumsily missed the .38 that I had tucked in my pants. But if he would have found a gun, I was prepared. I would have told the Colombians that anybody who would show up for a deal with strangers and didn't have a gun should get out of the business. At that point I would have begun walking out of the restaurant. Fortunately, it didn't have to go that far.

We conducted the normal back and forth negotiations. In an attempt to make me look more legitimate, I attempted to get a lower price than the $64,000 they had previously agreed upon. However, the Colombians wouldn't budge, so I finally agreed to meet them in the parking lot of the restaurant to conduct the deal, car to car. This deal, like all the other deals I had mentioned, appeared to have gone very smoothly during the negotiation stages, but it was anything but smooth because of the Colombians' paranoia and being in a strange city.

I finally convinced them to meet me in the parking lot where I would show one of them the money. The two Colombians and I walked out of the restaurant, but one of the guys went with me to my car. I popped the trunk and quickly displayed to him the $64,000.

This was by far the most dangerous part of the transaction and both the surveillance agents and I keenly focused on the actions and demeanor of the Colombian. In the event this was a rip-off, I had an obvious distress signal that could be seen by surveillance who could rush in and stop the theft.

Thankfully I didn't have to use the distress signal, closed the trunk of the car and followed the Colombian to another car in the parking lot that supposedly contained the cocaine. This was the second most dangerous part of the deal because at this

point the Columbian could have easily pulled a gun, shove me into my car, and steal the keys of the car that contained the $64,000.

Upon arriving at the Columbians' car, I saw the Colombian male I had previously met in the restaurant and a female sitting in the car which now presented three defendants instead of two. That wasn't a big issue as long as they had the cocaine. The Columbian that I was with said something in Spanish to his partners who immediately retrieved a bag from the floor of the front seat, rolled down the window, and showed me what looked like a package containing a kilogram of cocaine.

After smelling the contents of the package and detecting a slight smell of ether, I indicated that I was ready to do the deal and that they should come to my car. As is usual, they demanded that I go get the money and bring the money to their car. We went back and forth for a few minutes until I finally said that if they didn't bring the cocaine to my car, I was going to leave, and they could deal with somebody else.

Knowing that they had nobody else in Milwaukee and had no other options other than leaving, I figured I was in a good position to make demands. Once again greed took over, and they both agreed to accompany me to my car. More importantly, they agreed to bring the kilo of cocaine, which was in a brown paper shopping bag. This was the third most dangerous part of the deal because either of the parties could still pull a stick up of either the cocaine or the money.

My car was parked close by so again even though it looked like a legitimate deal, everybody involved was on high alert, especially the Colombians because in their minds I could still be the police and this could be a bust. Because the team and I knew that the Colombians would be very guarded, it was important for

the arrest team to get to my car at the same time the Columbians and I did.

While the two Colombians and I were walking to my car, ostensibly to get the $64,000, I gave a sign to the surveillance agents indicating it was Game Time and to move in and assist me with the arrest. As I saw the surveillance agents quickly approaching my position, I took a couple quick steps back from the Columbians, drew my service revolver and announced that I was the police and for them to get their hands up. Simultaneous with the action at my car, several surveillance cars converged in the restaurant parking lot, engines roaring and tires squealing to assist with the arrests and seizure of cocaine.

Both of the Colombian males and the female were arrested, taken downtown and processed by DEA and federal marshals. I didn't recall the disposition of this case but knew that the Colombians didn't cooperate, were convicted and sentenced to prison.

37

New Agent In the Office

In the spring of '84, my supervisor announced that a new agent was joining the squad. Agents were drowning in work in the Milwaukee office, and any extra pair of hands was welcome. On this particular day, the newest addition strolled in. I was called into the boss's office to meet the newbie. During the late '70s and early '80s new agents in Milwaukee were a rarity but this was the beginning of a hiring spree perpetuated by the cocaine crisis.

I walked to the boss's office, expecting the usual Miami Vice type of guy. Lo and behold, there stood a tall, dark-haired lady, looking as if she just stepped out of a teenage crime drama! My brain, clearly caught off guard, managed to blurt out, "It's a girl?" The extra pair of hands also came with fingernail polish!

Back then, female DEA agents were as rare as a polite telemarketer. In fact, up until the point of Jeanne's entry into the Milwaukee office, I had only met two female agents, one in Chicago and one in San Diego. I had mistakenly assumed our new recruit would be another mustached agent, but life, it seems, had different plans. The suits had decided they needed a feminine touch in our crime-fighting group. The Special Agent in Charge of FBI Milwaukee once charged that DEA Milwaukee was an irreverent group of cowboys.

As Jeanne got her feet wet on the job, she displayed an outstanding aptitude for all aspects of being a DEA agent: undercover work, report writing, testifying, surveillance, working with state and local law enforcement officers and later on managing an office full of DEA agents, local police and local sheriffs' deputies. Who would have thought? She might have been the only agent that I knew who received 20 of the highest annual evaluations in a row that we can receive in DEA.

Looking back 40 years, I was sure glad that she became an agent because Jeanne turned out to be an outstanding wife, stepmother, grandmother and sister-in-law. Jeanne also turned out to be an outstanding street agent and ultimately a very successful DEA supervisor.

38
Keep Moving Forward

During sometime in late 1985 Jeanne got an informant who was able to introduce her to a very well-known cocaine trafficker just south of Milwaukee. He bragged to the informant that he was capable of delivering multi-kilogram quantities of cocaine straight from Miami at a reasonable price. Jeanne instructed the informant to meet with the dealer, Rayburn Hendrix, and tell Rayburn that the informant had a customer who could purchase multi kilogram quantities of cocaine. Rayburn was a little thrown back when he was also told that the customer was a female.

Being greedy, Rayburn told the informant that he would meet the new customer, but she would have to show him that she had the money to back up the mouth. Arrangements were made for Jeanne, using the undercover name of Karen, to meet Rayburn at his home and flash $500,000. (a flash is nothing more than a display of money to a dealer to prove the veracity of the agent.) The informant was grilled making sure there were no holes in his story and verifying every little bit of information he offered up.

Arrangements made for the informant and Karen to travel to Rayburn's residence. The plan was for the informant and

Karen to enter the residence and make sure that only Rayburn was home and after that was accomplished, Karen would go to her OGV and retrieve two suitcases containing the half million dollars. Surveillance had been established on Rayburn's house long before Karen's arrival to ensure that there were no other actors involved.

Karen and the informant arrived at Rayburn's home, knocked on the door and were allowed in. After Karen and the informant got as good a look as they could of the inside of Rayburn's house, Karen excused herself and retrieved the half million dollars. Karen, letting herself into Rayburn's house, confidently walked into the living room and told Rayburn he could take a look at the money to ensure that she was for real. Rayburn opened one suitcase and took a look at the $100 bills. He then told Karen he wouldn't have to see the rest of the money because he believed that she was for real.

While the above was occurring the surveillance agents scattered inconspicuously throughout Rayburn's neighborhood were on pins and needles. There was nothing at all to prevent Rayburn from robbing Karen. All the necessary precautions had been taken as well as the unusual tactic of wiring Karen up.

Unfortunately, if something bad happened no matter how fast the surveillance agents moved in, it would come down to Karen and the informant fighting off Rayburn until backup arrived. Karen, as with all agents, had been trained for this possibility and was certainly mentally prepared for it. Fortunately, she didn't have to resort to her training.

After Rayburn inspected the contents of one of the suitcases, Karen told Rayburn that she needed ten kilos of cocaine delivered as soon as possible and asked Rayburn for his telephone number so she could contact him directly. As planned, the informant

strongly objected, but Karen on no uncertain terms, told him to shut up and that he would be taken care of and would not be cut out of the deal.

As planned, the informant meekly demurred to Karen's strong admonition and stormed out of Rayburn's house. Knowing that greed had overtaken Rayburn's natural reflexes, after the informant left, Karen told him that the informant would no longer be involved, and it was just going to be Karen, her partner and Rayburn involved in the deal.

Not too long after the above meetup, Karen called up Rayburn and ordered a half pound sample of cocaine. Arrangements were made for the meeting and on the given time and date Karen met Rayburn at a location just off of I-94 on Milwaukee's South Side. Because Rayburn was so convinced by the groundwork laid by the informant and by Karen's performance, he didn't even ask to see the money and just walked over to Karen's car and handed her the half pound of cocaine. Much to Rayburn's surprise, Karen gave the arrest signal, and Rayburn was taken into custody without incident.

Before the handcuffs were locked on Rayburn's wrist, the team knew he was going to cooperate, so they treated him with kid gloves. I was driving, and Karen was a passenger on the way to the Milwaukee office for processing the prisoner. Rayburn couldn't help himself and started, before being asked, giving names and numbers of his Miami sources of supply. Because Karen and I didn't have any notepads in the OGV, we had to keep asking him to slow down until they got to the office so an accurate report could be written.

When we got to the Milwaukee office, Karen started taking copious notes while I was calling a contact in Miami with the names and phone numbers of Rayburn's sources of supply.

Karen asked and received permission from the U.S. attorney's office not to charge Rayburn at that point and to allow us to play out the Miami deal. Eventually Karen ended the debriefing of Rayburn. She also instructed Rayburn on how he was going to handle introducing Karen to the Colombians either on the phone or in Miami.

Periodically I stuck my head in the debriefing but soon realized Rayburn didn't need any additional convincing. To say the least, Rayburn was greatly relieved that he wasn't going to be charged and going to jail that day. To make sure that Rayburn was truthful with his statements, Karen instructed him to call the Colombians and see if they had any product available. Karen also instructed Rayburn to tell the Colombians that he would place a large order in the near future if they were able to deliver.

During the initial telephone conversation, Rayburn told the Colombians that he was going to meet a money person and probably place an order for a large amount of cocaine. Karen had Rayburn place another call to the Colombians from the Milwaukee office undercover telephone. During the call Rayburn told the Colombians that his person was a female who had shown him a large amount of cash, a half a million dollars.

The Colombian started asking Rayburn all kinds of questions about this mysterious female. Fortunately, Rayburn had been briefed well enough so he had all the right answers. One of the answers which was critical was that Rayburn had dealt with this female on numerous occasions and trusted her implicitly. Breaking the ice for the introduction of a second agent, Rayburn told the Colombians that the female who would be doing the deal was backed by a guy that was 'hooked.' (Slang term for connected to the underworld)

191

The Colombians told Rayburn that they would talk about it and get back with him as to whether or not they would commit to doing the deal. Rayburn emphasized that the Colombians shouldn't waste any time because Karen was not used to waiting and had other people she could go to if she became impatient. Because Karen didn't know how long it would take for Rayburn to receive a phone call from the Colombians, she gave him a recorder with some tapes and told him to record any phone calls he received from the Columbians and to preserve the tapes.

A day later Rayburn received a telephone call from the Colombians and was told that if his people showed up in Miami with the money they would have as much cocaine as they wanted to buy. As Karen instructed, Rayburn told the Colombians he would need a couple days to get everything together and that Karen could meet them at a hotel at the Miami Airport and do the deal.

Again, as instructed by Karen, Rayburn called the Colombians back and told them he would not be able to make it for two weeks because of an unexpected family emergency. (This simply was Karen's attempt to avoid Rayburn being involved in any aspect of the deal. Plus, the Columbians could rationalize it and figure on more profits if they didn't have to pay Rayburn.)

The Colombians had enough faith in Rayburn that they told him to have his friend call the Colombians directly and make the final arrangements for the transaction. Knowing that once again greed would obscure clear judgment, Karen got together with Rayburn who placed a phone call to the Colombians.

After brief introductions were made, Rayburn put Karen on the phone who then scheduled to meet the Colombians on a Thursday night. Physical descriptions were exchanged, as well as the type of clothes that were going to be worn, and the time was set for 4 p.m. Thursday night at the airport hotel in the lobby.

As fate would have it, the Colombians said they couldn't do it on Thursday night but could on Friday night. Once again, we had to enlist a Miami Group to work another Friday night. Karen contacted the Miami DEA and briefed them about the proposed deal. The deal the Colombians agreed to was going to be for ten kilos. Between Karen and me, everything was set on Miami's end, and the only thing left was showing up and doing the deal. It was much easier said than done!

As a side note, Karen's brother Tom was the general manager of a large upscale hotel in Miami. When Karen knew that she and I were going to be traveling to Miami, she contacted her brother who arranged for two hotel rooms for the agents and one adjoining undercover hotel room in case it was necessary to receive phone calls or have the dealers deliver the cocaine to the room.

As I later found out, Tom only made one request in return for arranging the three hotel rooms: "Please don't have a bunch of cops with guns drawn arresting people in the lobby and making a big scene." Karen told Tom that it would be no problem figuring they would do the deal in the hotel parking lot or in the undercover room. I didn't anticipate any problems with that arrangement and was becoming more and more convinced that Karen was going to turn out to be a really good DEA agent.

Karen didn't tell the Colombians that I would be coming to Miami with her. That was going to be a surprise. Karen and I caught an early flight to Miami and checked in with the Miami DEA contact when we landed. Karen was informed that the Miami surveillance team would be in place at 3:30. Details were worked out regarding an arrest signal or a distress signal and what the limitations would be on Karen's and my movements.

Just prior to 4:00 p.m. the surveillance team radioed Karen, who was in the undercover room and advised her that two Colombian males fitting the description of the drug dealers had entered the lobby and were sitting on a sofa directly across the check-in desk. Karen and I took a deep breath and jumped on the elevator down to the lobby.

As soon as the elevator hit the lobby floor, the doors opened, and Karen and I could see the Colombians seated on the couch off to the right. Although Karen made eye contact with the Colombians, they seemed to pretend as if they hadn't seen her. That of course was because they were expecting to meet a tall, dark-haired female who was not accompanied by a man. Expecting this reaction, Karen (SA Jeanne) and I confidently walked up to the Colombians and introduced ourselves, indicating that we were Rayburn's friends from Wisconsin.

The Colombians appeared to be nervous and did very little talking until Karen told them that I was her partner and that she was of the understanding that Rayburn had already told them about Karen's partner. Still having shoulder length hair, a beard and a brown floppy hat, I sat down in the chair adjacent to the couch. Karen had already taken a seat on the opposite side of where I was sitting. The Colombians acknowledged that Rayburn had told them about Karen's partner but didn't tell them that he would be involved in the transaction.

Remaining silent up until this point, I felt it necessary to jump into the conversation. First of all, I asked the Colombians if they had names. "No" was their expected response. Slightly agitated, I responded, "That's funny because most of the Colombians we deal with in Florida have names." Then trying to lower the temperature, I said, "Okay. But did you think that Karen was going to come to Miami with $300,000 by herself?"

Then with a voice that was slightly raised, I asked point blank, "How many times have you dealt with Benny?" (Karen had previously instructed Rayburn not to answer his phone at all on Friday night.) When they didn't answer, I said that apparently, they hadn't dealt with him enough because it sure seemed that they didn't trust him.

The Colombians looked at each other. At this point Karen, raising her hand and voice, pointed at the big Colombian who didn't have a name, and said that she and I were going to go up to the room to get the money and bring it back to the lobby, and that she expected that they would get the dope and do the same. "No, No, No!!!" was all they heard from the big guy.

Once again, I felt compelled to join in the verbal fray. I left my seat and walked over to the big Colombian, bent a little bit so I was face to face and simply stated, "Look, if you don't follow through with the delivery as promised, we're not going to waste any more time."

Knowing what was coming, Karen stood up, waiting for me to finish before she started walking toward the elevator. Before she was out of hearing range of the Colombians she said, "Come on, Bill, these guys are a waste of time." I thought the Colombians were a little stunned because as we entered the elevators, I caught a quick glance of them still sitting on the couch involved in a deep conversation. Karen and I knew they had the room number of the undercover room, and there was a possibility that after they thought about it, they would try to contact us.

Both Karen and I felt completely comfortable with our undercover presentation but still made plans to fly home later that evening. After we got up to the undercover room, Jeanne called her brother Tom and asked if he wanted to come up to the room and have a beer. While Jeanne was talking to her brother, I

contacted the group that was on surveillance and told them that the deal was a no-go and thanked them for their help. Thankfully they were gracious because most of them were still able to get home by 5:30 p.m.

While Jeanne was talking to her brother Tom, she also asked him to bring a six-pack of Heineken. Tom was up in the room within 15 minutes carrying an ice cold six pack of Heineken. He had watched the meeting break up in the lobby and assumed that he needed to be ready. Jeanne and Tom talked while I, having not much to add, focused on not letting the Heineken get warm.

After about an hour passed, the undercover telephone rang in the room. Karen (SA Jeanne) answered and was told "We got it."

Jumping back into her undercover persona Karen asked, "Who's got what?"

The knucklehead on the phone simply said, "It's me, you know, from downstairs."

Karen knowing that the surveillance group was probably home by now was locked on the horns of a dilemma. Karen knew she had to buy time to allow the surveillance team to set up again in the lobby. After a slight hesitation Karen asked, "How many?"

No name answered, "Three, and after that's done seven more" meaning they had three kilos of cocaine and after that deal was successfully completed, they could deliver seven more. Karen told no name to hold on, she had to talk to her partner. Purposely not cupping the phone Karen relayed the new information to me.

In an agitated voice I replied to Karen that the guy had just gotten to his motel with the money and it would take him an hour to get back. At this point Karen and I were just trying to buy time to gather up a surveillance team. I said in a voice loud enough for no name to hear. "Tell them to be here in an hour and 15 minutes and to have the dope or don't show up at all."

Now for whatever reason no name became very compliant and said they would be on time with the three kilos. Of course, Karen and I didn't believe that, but now we had the Colombians eating out of our hands and were much closer to a successful deal. While Karen was still on the phone with the Colombians, I ran back into the adjoining room and quickly called the supervisor of the surveillance team. Without divulging what the supervisor said, he agreed to put together a team and be ready at the appointed time. He wasn't happy and rightfully so. I certainly couldn't blame him, three kilos to the Miami agents wasn't much of a deal.

After being advised by the surveillance team that they were set up and prepared for the meeting between Karen and me and the Columbians, Karen told the Miami agents to advise once the Colombians entered the lobby. The ball was now in our court and we didn't want to look anxious or enthusiastic to the Colombians. At exactly the appointed time, the surveillance team observed the two Colombians carrying an athletic bag enter and take a seat in a different area of the lobby. As the surveillance team was notifying us, one of the Colombians got up to walk to a house phone and called the undercover room.

Karen answered the phone and was told "We got it. Were in the lobby."

Karen simply responded, "Five minutes" and hung up the phone, giving me a thumbs up. Simultaneously, I was contacting the surveillance team from the adjoining room that the Colombians said they had the coke. The surveillance team relayed that they had observed the Colombians carrying some type of athletic bag. We then agreed that once we got to the lobby, we would insist on seeing the coke, presumably contained in the bag, and then give the surveillance team an arrest signal.

Knowing that it was game time, thoughts raced through both our heads that the athletic bag could contain guns and that there was nothing to prevent a quick robbery which of course would end very poorly for the Colombians and maybe us. But there was still that chance. One last quick communication with the surveillance team, and we descended down to the lobby. Once eye contact was made, we made our way to the two Colombians and the mysterious athletic bag.

We were carrying a small suitcase stuffed with books, (supposed to be money) sat down adjacent to the Colombians and asked if they were ready. The athletic bag which was at the feet of the big Colombian was kicked over to Karen who instinctively unzipped it in a cautious manner and took a quick look. Karen smelled the tell-tale odor of cocaine and saw the three brick size packages. In the meantime, I was pretending to scan the lobby area for the police. Karen simply said, "Looks good" and as previously planned with the surveillance team, I took off my brown hat and slid the suitcase to the smaller Colombian.

Before the Colombian was able to open the suitcase, Karen and I quickly stood up and took a few steps back while at the same time drawing our weapons, giving the arrest team plenty of room in the event of resistance. There was no resistance, and the arrest went off without incident. From the time my hat went off until the two Colombians were hustled out to the parking lot and shoved into two OGV'S, about a minute or less had transpired. A quick field test was performed on some residual powder in the bottom of the athletic bag confirming that they had three kilos of cocaine.

The Miami agents were now responsible for processing the cocaine, the prisoners, and locating the missing seven kilos of coke while Karen and I had to return to Milwaukee to write a

report. I thanked the supervisor of the surveillance/arrest team who again was very gracious but requested that I should avoid Fridays the next time a Miami trip was planned. I don't know what happened to the two Colombians and never bothered to get their names except for the reports. Later I received a phone call from a Miami agent who told me that these two Colombians invited some rivals on a one-way fishing charter. The rivals ended up as shark bait several miles offshore.

Before completing her notes on the deal and flying back to peaceful Milwaukee, Karen had to deal with one more issue. She had assured her brother Tom, the general manager of the hotel where the deal occurred, that there would be no visible police presence. Technically, DEA agents dressed in full tactical gear with handguns drawn are really federal agents, so therefore there was no police presence. That's how Karen explained the situation to Tom who was upset for a while but very soon forgot it had ever happened, as long as Karen was safe.

39

Iran Contras In Milwaukee?

During the fall of 1986 an informant introduced me to a Nicaraguan, Detlaf Thomas, who allegedly was dealing huge quantities of cocaine and had access to tons of it. After the initial introduction, I felt very comfortable that the meeting with Thomas was successful and that Thomas was comfortable dealing with me.

I was able to pull Thomas aside and tell him I didn't want the informant involved in any of our deals because he would scrape too much money off the top. Thomas agreed, and the informant was discreetly cut out of the deal. The informant knew that he was going to be cut out and was instructed to resist any type of conversation leaning in that direction in order to make it more realistic.

During the first couple meetings which occurred in southside Milwaukee bars located just out of downtown Milwaukee, I purchased ounce quantities of cocaine from Thomas. He seemed relaxed during the meetings. During the second or third meeting with him, I introduced him to the new agent in the office, Special Agent Jeanne Tasch who was introduced using the undercover

name, Karen. She was introduced as my financial partner and therefore had some say in how we conducted business.

Karen was introduced to Thomas because I knew we were going to start talking about substantial kilogram quantities of cocaine and instead of having another agent show up late in the game, it was better to see how he reacted in the initial meeting. Thomas had no problem meeting Karen, nor did he have a problem discussing cocaine transactions in front of her. After the second buy we began negotiating for a much larger quantity of cocaine.

Karen and I told Thomas that before we got into the multi-kilo cocaine range, we wanted to purchase a quarter pound of cocaine from him and make sure that the quality remained as high as the previous two purchases. Arrangements were made to meet Thomas at another South Side Milwaukee bar after we haggled a little bit over the price of the quarter pound. Finally, Thomas agreed that he would sell us a quarter pound of cocaine for $1,200 an ounce.

Prior to the transaction, surveillance was established in the vicinity of the bar where we were supposed to meet. After surveillance was established, we entered the bar and greeted Thomas who had already arrived. Greetings were exchanged, and I asked him if he had the dope and was pleased when he said he did. He was one of the first drug dealers that I had ever dealt with who was always on time, always had the package, and really didn't create any grief about doing the deal. The reason for this was because the informant was very good and followed directions to the T, even when we instructed him to contact Thomas between deals.

Obviously, Thomas asked if I had the money, and I replied that the money was in my car and that Karen would go to the

car to retrieve it. Thomas left the bar and retrieved the cocaine from his car, as observed by surveillance agents, and Karen left the bar to retrieve the cash. The exchange of the cocaine and cash occurred in the pool room after which Karen left the bar ostensibly to test the cocaine and make sure it was pure.

After Karen performed the chemical field test, she returned to the bar and indicated that the cocaine was excellent. Of course, Thomas had already gone to the men's room to count the money in order to make sure that it was right. When Thomas returned to the pool room, we started negotiating for larger quantities of cocaine, the first of which would be around six kilos for which he didn't have any problem. Simultaneous with the negotiations, Thomas was unusually distracted by what was on the TV news that night. He was so distracted that I mentioned that to him, and he responded that he was very interested in the news broadcast.

Taking a step back, during this time period, political strife erupted in Nicaragua caused by the CIA's involvement with a group of anti-government rebels referred to as the CONTRAS. The CONTRAS were attempting to overthrow the Nicaraguan government and were being funded by the CIA. Allegations were made that the CIA was turning a blind eye and allowing the CONTRAS to sell drugs in order to raise money to purchase weapons for their fight.

Clearly Thomas was upset regarding the Nicaraguan situation and made it no secret that he supported the CONTRAS and their efforts to overthrow the Sandinistas, who controlled the government. Thomas's visceral, and most importantly, spontaneous reaction to the newscast convinced me that at least his feelings were sincere.

At one point during negotiations Thomas indicated that

he sent a large portion of his profits from selling cocaine to the CONTRA rebels keeping the remaining funds as living expenses. Later it struck me as being an odd statement under the circumstances. Thomas just completed a drug transaction and the possibility of getting busted or ripped off still lingered, and all he could think about was politics. There was none of the paranoia or edginess that was common when dealers were selling drugs to fairly new clients.

After completing the transaction and having another drink to our future success, Karen and I returned to the office, processed the cocaine, and completed some reports. The next day I relayed the above information to the prosecutor in charge of the case who appeared skeptical of the CONTRA story. Even though I felt there was truth to the story, I didn't see any sense in pursuing it.

I figured if everything went right, once Thomas was arrested, he could provide the information about the CONTRAS and the money if it was true. However, everything Thomas said and the way he said it coupled with his body mannerisms caused me to believe there was at least partial truth in his story. The prosecutor on the other hand had an opposite opinion and did not believe that Thomas was part of the CONTRA movement. We both respected each other's opinions and had worked cases together for several years.

Having previously agreed that we would lay low during the holiday season, attempts to contact Thomas during early 1987 were futile. Based on his previous behavior, this caused me some concern. I reached out to the original informant and had him contact Thomas's sister, Leticia, who remained in Wisconsin. Leticia was ambiguous with the informant and indicated that Thomas was not and would not be available for an unknown

amount of time. Thomas had previously mentioned his sister and brother, Juan, as had the informant during the briefings with Karen and me.

Because Thomas had been so responsive and prompt on other occasions, this information led me to believe that he had been spooked either by me or another one of his customers. Based on my gut feeling, I requested and received an arrest warrant for Thomas and when attempting to execute it determined that Thomas had fled. This was disheartening because I firmly believed that Thomas had bought Karen and me lock stock and barrel. After a short period of time, the U.S. Marshals were notified so that they could enter him in the appropriate apprehension systems.

Figuring that we were done with this case, we were surprised when Leticia reached out to the original informant and said she would be traveling to Miami in the near future and returning with a large quantity of cocaine. This dispelled any thoughts that Thomas's meeting with Karen and me had caused any paranoia. This was particularly surprising because any suspicions that I had about bringing the heat on Thomas were erased. We instructed the informant to try to narrow the time frame down when Leticia would return.

Not long after the informant spoke to Leticia, he was contacted by Leticia and provided a specific time when she and the cocaine would be in Wisconsin. Close to that time frame the informant was contacted by Leticia indicating she had returned to Wisconsin and had the cocaine if the informant wanted to buy any. The informant indicated that Thomas' friend, that being me, might be interested, and the informant would be back in touch with the order.

It now made complete sense that Karen and I weren't the reasons Thomas disappeared because Leticia absolutely knew that the informant introduced us to her brother. Furthermore, during meetings with Thomas, he indicated that his cocaine business was a family affair involving his brother and sister. The reason Thomas disappeared still remained a mystery. Several years later when I was assigned to the New Orleans Division office, Thomas was arrested by DEA, Miami based on information from an informant that he was in possession of a large quantity of cocaine. No cocaine was seized at the time of his arrest.

Returning to Leticia and the cocaine trip, DEA started a loose surveillance on the address that was believed where the cocaine would be stored by Leticia. After gathering enough information to apply for a search warrant, SA Jeanne (Karen) got the warrant and returned to the residence to execute it. Surveillance was maintained on the house while getting the search warrant in the event somebody tried to leave. If that were the case, the vehicle would be stopped and any occupants identified. After receiving the search warrant, it was executed during the very early morning hours in March 1987.

Found hidden in a car parked in the garage of Thomas's residence were 2 kilos of cocaine. The occupants of the home were Leticia and Miami residents Gustavo Romo and Luiba Sainz. Go figure, two people from Miami showed up at the same time a large quantity of cocaine was supposed to arrive. All three were arrested without incident based on the totality of the circumstances involving the discovery of the two kilograms of cocaine. The cocaine just happened to be stashed in the pant legs of a pair of Romo's pants which were located in a suitcase that was stored in the car in the garage.

Although disappointed that they did not reach their objective of identifying Detlaf's source of supply and confirming his story about the Contras, SA Jeanne and I could at least be satisfied

that we cut off a cocaine pipeline from Miami to Milwaukee. Ultimately the charges against Romo were dropped in return for his cooperation, and both Leticia and Luiba went to trial, were convicted and sentenced to prison.

Neither lady offered to cooperate, and Romo turned out to have been duped by Leticia. What developed pending Leticia's trial was that she claimed to have been the love partner of the National Security Commander of the Nicaraguan Samoza regime. Samoza's reign ended in 1979 when the Sandinistas took charge.

As a reminder, the CONTRAS were fighting the Sandinistas, allegedly with money and weapons derived from the cocaine trade and the CIA. This case developed no direct evidence linking drugs, weapons and money to the CONTRAS other than the claims of Detlaf and Leticia.

I could never understand why Detlaf literally disappeared sometime after the four-ounce cocaine transaction. That would make complete sense if Detlaf knew Karen and I were police. But that argument fell flat because when Leticia was getting cocaine from Miami, she contacted the original informant who she knew was involved in the four-ounce cocaine deal involving both Karen and me.

Likewise, evidence revealed that Detlaf traveled freely, using his own passport, between Nicaragua and Miami while he was a federal fugitive? Although Thomas was arrested by Miami DEA agents because of the outstanding Milwaukee warrant, he appeared before a federal magistrate and was released on bond. The reason Thomas was arrested was because DEA Miami received information from a reliable informant that he was in Miami dealing large quantities of cocaine.

My experience with fugitives was that once becoming a fugitive and subsequently caught, this person would be locked

up until trial. Even more puzzling was the fact that after he was released from Miami, he appeared voluntarily in Milwaukee federal court to answer to the cocaine distribution charges, and again he was released. Detlaf's release in Milwaukee could be explained because he turned himself in and because the magistrate in Milwaukee was following the lead of the magistrate in Miami.

What makes no sense was that Detlaf traveled to Milwaukee from Miami to answer to the Milwaukee cocaine distribution charges. He did so voluntarily, but then walked out of the Milwaukee Courthouse and disappeared off the face of the earth. I couldn't even speculate on why the events unfolded the way they did. I could only conclude that from the time Detlaf disappeared in Milwaukee the first time, until the time he walked out of federal court in Milwaukee, a black hole of information and unusual events surrounds that time period.

40

Sad Goodbye

Augie, who was my original partner in Milwaukee and who had convinced me to transfer to Milwaukee, took a transfer and went to Quito, Ecuador. After a short stint in Ecuador, Augie had to return to the states because he severely injured a leg while jumping out of a helicopter during an enforcement effort. He was transferred to Minneapolis as a group supervisor and reconnected with me exchanging weekly phone calls and updates on each other.

I thought that Augie sounded great, happy to be back in the U.S., and enjoying his new supervisory position. While on surveillance with MKE 14, (SA Jeanne) one day close to the holidays during the early 2000s I heard the familiar, "Milwaukee Base to MKE 10."

I responded, "Go for MKE 10 Milwaukee base."

"Are you driving or stationary?"

I replied, "I'm mobile."

Base, giving a very unusual command, "Pull over and park and acknowledge when parked."

That command was so unusual that I grabbed the first parking spot I could and transmitted to base, "I'm stationary, go ahead with your transmission."

208

After a brief pause and in a voice that was crackling with anxiety the base operator simply indicated, "MKE 7 is dead." A gut punch . . . Augie had been assigned to Milwaukee for so many years and was still routinely referred to as MKE 7. Ironically, I was parked across the street from a popular Brady Street watering hole and immediately transmitted to the base operator, "I'll be 10-7" or in layman's terms out of service. Without having to tell base where I was, they knew it was in a bar. That's where agents grieved.

Later, after returning to reality, I determined that Augie had died from a massive heart attack while celebrating Christmas with his family. He was in his early forties. The funeral was held in Chicago and on the night before the funeral, Augie's wife met me in a bar with a bunch of other agents from Minneapolis and Chicago who had worked with him. A mutual friend had agreed to do the eulogy, but unfortunately, he was stranded in San Francisco and would be unable to make the funeral. So, I was asked to pinch hit and accepted the request more out of obligation then desire.

That evening and early the next morning I put together some notes. The next morning when it was time for me to deliver the eulogy, I slowly walked to the front of the church, turned around and the only thing I saw or remembered was Augie's wife and young children, a boy and a girl, sitting in the front pew. They were staring at me as if they were pleading for this tragedy to be over. I couldn't help. Tom Stacy aka Augie was a great friend and great partner. MKE 7 was 10-7

41
More Sorrow

During the late 1980s Mel transferred to Quantico, Virginia, and became a key member of DEA's international training team. He traveled all over the world teaching our foreign counterparts' various aspects of drug law enforcement including working undercover, handling informants and conducting surveillance. Thankfully I was invited to teach at two DEA classes conducted in Bangkok, Thailand, and Lima, Peru. During those courses when we were not teaching, we got to see a lot of both of those countries, and it was a great experience.

Mel and I stayed in very close touch during his whole stint at Quantico with the exception of when he was traveling overseas. My sister moved with Mel to Quantico with her daughter. It was funny how a half pound cocaine deal with a biker spun my sister's life around and caused her to pick up and leave her hometown with my fishing buddy. Eventually Mel moved back to Chicago with my sister but still had failed to make her an honest woman.

After Mel moved back to Chicago, he telephoned me and asked if I wanted to meet him and my sister in Las Vegas. After checking with my wife Jeanne, we made final arrangements to meet in Las Vegas. Mel told me during their final planning session

about the time of arrival, departure and accommodations where they were going to stay.

"Oh, by the way, bring a nice change of clothes because I'm going to marry your sister!"

"Okay then. See you in Vegas—and by the way, welcome to the family!"

Jeanne and I traveled to Las Vegas to watch my best friend marry my sister.

Sadly, the last time I saw Mel was when he and my sister traveled from their retirement home in Texas to Wisconsin to attend a surprise birthday party for my 60th birthday. I was surprised to say the least and as I was walking through the crowd shaking hands, I saw Mel sitting in the corner. When our eyes met, he gave me that patented gotcha smile that so many drug dealers had regretted seeing.

Mel returned to Texas and within a month he and Donna flew out to Vegas for a short vacation. While they were in Vegas, I received an early morning phone call from my sister who simply said, "He's gone."

My ignorant response was "where?" When Donna didn't respond and started crying, I knew what had happened and came very close to collapsing into a ball.

Although Mel's son had met him in Vegas for a wrestling match, Donna still needed support. Jeanne and I planned for various family members to travel to Vegas and support Donna as well as Mel's son. Jeanne and I decided it would be best to wait for Donna to get home when she was by herself and then fly down to Texas to help her recover.

Shortly after the phone call with Donna, my natural instincts caused me to call the Las Vegas office of The Drug Enforcement Administration and find out who the boss was to see if DEA

could provide some support until Donna returned to Texas. I was told the name of the boss, which shocked me, because he was a good friend of both Mel and I and had worked in Chicago for a number of years. I was told he was in a staff meeting and could not be disturbed. But after explaining the circumstances, within minutes Mike was on the phone asking what he could do.

I told him my sister's situation and where she was located and her phone number. His response was simple, "I'm on it. I'll personally take care of her for as long as necessary." Although neither Mel nor I had seen this guy for 10 years, the bond forged while in Chicago and Milwaukee was as strong as ever, and I would be forever indebted to him for his incredible support at a very bad time.

At Mel's funeral The Preacher, (aka The Old Ranger, aka Zippers) and I each delivered a eulogy. The Old Rangers eulogy began with these exact words, "Mel . . . Mel, what have you done to us now?"

My first words in the eulogy "The White Prince of Peace and happiness is 10-7." Besides that, the only thing that I remembered about the eulogy was looking out and seeing my sister jump in my wife's lap, sobbing uncontrollably and Mel's two grown children staring at me with the same look that Augie's kids had. Cause of death, heart attack. A more loyal friend no man can have.

42

No Words Could Describe the Depravity

On February 9, 2024, I attended a memorial service for a wonderful, kind woman in a nearby city. After the service a relative mentioned a double homicide which had recently occurred and questioned how anybody could just pull the trigger and kill completely innocent people. We discussed that subject for a short while but on the way home, I remembered something that occurred in one of the cases I worked on which raised the same question.

During December 1987 a 10-year-old boy, his mother and father were brutally murdered in a Northwestern suburb of Milwaukee. The murders occurred within minutes of each other and were committed by more than one person.

The homicide investigation determined that all three of the victims knew their assailants. So conversely, the assailants knew who they were going to kill and had some kind of relationship with the deceased.

Several stark pieces of evidence remained scattered on the floor when the bodies were discovered. The court records and DEA reports of the investigation, generated after the arrest of

the father, Michael Drobec showed that the arrest occurred after the delivery of a pound of cocaine to a DEA informant by Drobec and an associate.

Taking a look back, months before the murder, a DEA informant was approached by an individual who said he could arrange for a one-pound cocaine deal. The informant contacted DEA who instructed him to go ahead and set up the deal. The informant also told DEA that the source of supply for the cocaine was a guy with the nickname 'Rerun' and also a member of a prominent Milwaukee motorcycle gang. Rerun was identified as a guy by the name of Michael Drobec who had a lengthy criminal record including a stint in prison.

DEA arranged for the deal at the given time and date. Surveillance on the locations DEA thought would be used by the dealers during the transaction was established. Surveillance agents saw the guy, who was the ultimate source of supply, put a box in Drobec's car. Based on the arrangements made for the deal, DEA knew that the box contained cocaine. DEA also observed a passenger in Drobec's car.

When Drobec delivered the cocaine to a middleman, DEA made the decision to arrest the people involved in the deal. When approaching the car occupied by Drobec and his passenger, they both started leaning forward as if they were grabbing something under their car seats which immediately indicated that they were reaching for guns. At a moment like this, a thousand thoughts raced through each agent's minds as they approached the vehicle.

The first thought was to shoot or not to shoot in that split second. If the decision was to shoot, what kind of shot was available from the position the agent was in? Were there any pedestrians in close proximity that could be hit, any other agents

in a position where they might be hit? Any houses that a stray bullet might find its way into? Exactly at the same time with these thoughts racing through the agents' minds, they were all hollering "Don't do it" and "Put your hands where I can see them" and "Freeze. Don't move" in unison.

The decision not to shoot was a walk in the park compared to the decision to shoot. Fortunately for everybody involved, both dealers froze as directed, very slowly raised their hands and complied with each subsequent command. "Keep your hands in the air where I can see them!"

"Don't make another move!"

"We won't hesitate to shoot."

The agents convinced them to sit up with their hands in the air and give it up instead of the other option which would have been fatal for both of them. At the same time, they both raised their hands, the agents rushed to the car doors, quickly pulled them open and pulled them out of the car and onto the ground. DEA also seized the one pound of cocaine that had been negotiated through the informant. As expected, under the seats were a two-shot Derringer and a cocked .9 mm semi-automatic handgun. Perched between them was a police scanner which of course gave them a false sense of security because they could not monitor DEA channels.

Ironically while they being processed, neither one of them indicated any desire to cooperate and gave DEA the impression they were going to fight the charges tooth and nail. During November of 1987, Drobec pled guilty in federal court to possession with intent to distribute and conspiracy to distribute one pound of cocaine in addition to possession of a firearm by a convicted felon. One month later he along with his wife and child were executed while at their home.

Three weeks after the triple homicide, an associate of Drobec and a person feared by the motorcycle gang to be in possession of information regarding the above homicides was found dead from an alleged overdose. The amount and mixture of the drugs in his system indicated that he most probably died of an intentional 'hot shot.' (A hot shot is when the drugs are put together before injection and are mixed in an extremely strong concentration purposely to kill the user) Dealing drugs often leads to collateral damage, enough said.

43

Miami Calls For Help

During November of 1988 a Miami agent, Richard, received information from an informant indicating that Colombian contacts in Milwaukee were interested in purchasing 15 kilos of cocaine. Over the next several days the informant negotiated the terms of the purchase with Andres Zuniga. At the same time, Special Agent Richard was coordinating activities with the Milwaukee resident office just the same as I had done with Miami on several occasions except in reverse. After everybody was on the same page, the informant and Special Agent Richard traveled to Milwaukee.

After meeting with the Milwaukee agents, Richard and the informant decided to meet with Zuniga and Sergio Aguero at an airport hotel in Milwaukee where Richard was staying. Surveillance between the Milwaukee PD and DEA was being coordinated. During this meeting agents from the Milwaukee resident office conducted surveillance and had adjoining rooms with Richard for his protection. After the meeting between Zuniga and Richard began, Zuniga told Richard that his money man was willing to pay $250,000 for the 15 kilos of cocaine. A white guy from Miami selling cocaine to a Colombian in Milwaukee was unusual to say the least.

A temporary problem arose when Zuniga indicated that his money man wanted one kilogram of cocaine fronted (given as a free sample to test its quality) before the deal could be completed. Richard told Zuniga that he wanted the money man to front some money to Richard before any deal could be completed. Negotiations were now at a standstill and Zuniga indicated that he would have to talk to his money man. Zuniga and Sergio Aguero then left the hotel and drove to a payphone where Milwaukee surveillance observed Aguero placing a phone call from a pay telephone.

After making a brief stop at Aguero's apartment, both Aguero and Zuniga returned to the room being occupied by the undercover Agent Richard, again while under the surveillance of Milwaukee agents and police. At Aguero's request, Richard showed a kilogram of cocaine to Aguero and Zuniga and allowed them to take a small sample for testing. (Just as in prior reverse undercover operations, Richard had received permission from DEA and the Department of Justice to release a small sample of cocaine.) After testing the cocaine, Aguero indicated that he liked its quality and that the money man lived approximately a half an hour from their current location.

Aguero told Richard that he would leave and meet with his money man in an attempt to receive enough money to buy the kilogram of cocaine he had just tested. Aguero indicated that he would not even be allowed to bring Zuniga to meet the money man. Zuniga was dropped off, and Aguero continued to an apartment building on South 113th Street in Milwaukee where he was observed by Milwaukee agents to be entering apartment number 2. (Although following people from one place to another sounds easy enough, it's very difficult to do in order not to expose the surveillance vehicles too many times.)

218

After a short period of time, Aguero left the apartment and picked up Zuniga, continuing to the undercover room occupied by special agent Richard. Aguero told Richard that the money man refused to advance any money and after negotiations seemed to reach a standstill, a decision was made to arrest Zuniga and Aguero. At about the same time, an individual identified as Luis Valencia left apartment number 2 and he too was followed by surveillance agents.

Milwaukee police officers were allowed by Valencia's girlfriend to enter the apartment and conduct a quick cursory search to make sure there were no other individuals in apartment number 2. At about the same time, other officers from the Milwaukee Police Department located Valencia, stopped and arrested him. After Valencia was transported to apartment number 2, he was offered all the appropriate warnings and through an interpreter gave permission to search his apartment.

Prior to the search however, Valencia admitted that he had about $9,000 in cash in the apartment along with the .357 Magnum revolver. After conducting a thorough search of the apartment, one more revolver was found but neither the Milwaukee police officers on the scene nor the DEA agents could locate a large enough amount of money that could be used to purchase the amount of cocaine that Aguero was negotiating with Richard. For a short while it seemed as if a lot of time and money had been wasted.

As most of the officers and agents were leaving apartment number 2, Larry DeValkenaere a member of Milwaukee's Tactical Squad, the 700s, and I remained at the doorway leading outside for no particular reason.

Just standing there looking around, Larry noticed a laundry room located just to the right of the exit door with a typical

washer and dryer and a large laundry basket full of dirty clothes. As Larry was gazing into the laundry room, he glanced up at Valencia and noticed that his demeanor changed from relaxed to nervous and agitated.

Because of this, and without saying a word, Larry began poking around in the laundry room and after failing to locate anything suspicious, turned over the laundry basket as the last futile attempt to find some evidence. Bingo!!!! Concealed under the soiled clothing was a mound of $100 bills. The dynamic of the search immediately changed from that of frustration to Miranda warnings for Valencia, Aguero and Zuniga were all transported to the Milwaukee DEA office for processing.

The $100 bills were counted by Larry and a DEA agent after which it was determined that there was about $320,000 which would have been more than enough to purchase the cocaine that Richard was allegedly offering to sell. Later, as in all cases, the money was taken to a bank and counted again with a money counting machine which verified the original count.

$328,000 seized during DEA/Milwaukee police operations

At the conclusion of a trial and appeals, the Seventh Circuit Court of Appeals affirmed Aguero's and Valencia's convictions and sentences. Without question the unique aspect of this investigation was the incredible undercover ability of the DEA agent from Miami who started the investigation. Richard successfully ended up posing as a cocaine distributor selling it to three Latin males. Instead of the Milwaukee agents going to Miami to get the cocaine, the Miami agents came to Milwaukee to get the money.

44

I Get Burned

As I approached my 22 or 23rd year milestone of working undercover in Milwaukee, the stakes kept rising, and so did my paranoia. Each deal became a high-wire act, balancing on the tightrope of not getting outed as a DEA agent. With every transaction, I had to be more careful, and my informant debriefings had to be tighter than a pair of skinny jeans on a hipster. To make matters worse, a bunch of defense attorneys in Milwaukee had begun warning their clients about anyone who looked even remotely like me. Imagine trying to blend in when my own likeness was the subject of a city-wide alert.

It was one particular undercover escapade that finally convinced me to hang up my undercover hat—or rather, my beard trimmers. I had just scored two ounces of cocaine from a mid-level dealer who, according to the intel, was supposed to be a goldmine of kilograms. And, even better, he didn't seem to be connected to any of the other lowlifes I had arrested. Just a day after this transaction, I received a phone call from Richard Forest, a local defense attorney with a knack for representing the less-than-savory.

The conversation started off with the usual pleasantries, but then Forest asked if I still had a beard. It was clear that this was not just a question about my grooming habits; it was more of a hint with a side of 'I'm about to blow your cover.' Trying to sound nonchalant, I responded with a cryptic, "Maybe I do, and maybe I don't." At the same time, I was mentally searching for a razor in the office. Forest, sensing that I was playing a game of undercover cat-and-mouse, decided to cut to the chase. He mentioned that one of his clients had walked into his office claiming to have sold cocaine to someone who looked a lot like a DEA agent.

Never one to back down from a challenge, I invited Forest and his client to the DEA office to discuss this conundrum. It was as if both of us were playing a game of 'I know you know I know,' with no winners in sight. By the end of the day, the client and Forest showed up at the DEA office. The client became an informant—albeit a rather unproductive one—but taught me a valuable lesson about knowing when to call it quits on my Milwaukee undercover escapades.

45

The Milwaukee Street Gang

Sometime during the latter part of 1989, I got a call from a Milwaukee police lieutenant who wondered if I could meet him and a captain from the Milwaukee Sheriff's Department for lunch at a restaurant on the South Side of Milwaukee. The meeting was set up and we had a good lunch. During the lunch I learned some very disturbing details about a particular gang that was working mostly on Milwaukee's North Side.

The most disturbing information relayed by the officers was that this particular gang was probably responsible for 40 drive-by shootings, some resulting in homicides. The gang also dealt in drugs, illegal firearms and receiving stolen property. I had been concentrating almost exclusively on Milwaukee's South Side and was totally ignorant about Milwaukee's North Side. To say the least, I was about to embark on an investigation that would consume me for 8 months.

I told the local guys I would be happy to look into it but wanted to make sure that I would have access to all city and county reports and evidence linked to the gang. They indicated that that wouldn't be a problem and within a week or two, my

office was full of hundreds of files linked to the gang. There was so much information that I had to initially sort through the information in a larger space in the U.S. attorney's office. Not long after I started skimming through the materials did, I realize that there was definitely a case to be made on the gang.

Because so much evidence linked the gang members together, which legally would be a conspiracy, 21 USC 846, I requested to be assigned an intelligence analyst from Chicago to help me sort through and make sense of all the files. It didn't take long for me to brief Assistant United States Attorney William Wags who I had worked many cases with before and respected not only his opinion but his drive to get the job done.

After Wags, his nickname, went through some of the evidence, he indicated to me that he too was satisfied that there was a case to be made, but because of the danger posed by this gang, he pushed for a wiretap. The reason for this was obvious. Gang members and other street dealers associated with the gang would be difficult if not impossible to turn into government witnesses unless it was an airtight case with a lot of prison time.

As luck would have it, during this process I arrested an individual who wanted to cooperate with the government and more importantly was a member of the gang, and believe it or not, was not afraid of them. After arresting this guy, I applied for and received a pen register order. A pen register is basically a device that records outgoing phone numbers from a specific telephone, in this case the president of the gang Sterling Daniels, aka ST.

It didn't take long to determine that although he was the president of the gang, he wasn't necessarily smart. He made hundreds of calls on a good day and because I could see the telephone number he was calling the DEA was able to determine

that almost all of his calls were going to known drug dealers. Without the complete cooperation of the Milwaukee Police Department, the Milwaukee County Sheriff's Department, the Wisconsin Department of Justice, and the Bureau of Alcohol Tobacco and Firearms a lot of the information gleaned from the pen register would have remained with the individual agencies. At the same time, I was using my new informant to make small buys off of the smaller dealers in the gang.

As the pen register was spitting out numbers, and the intelligence analyst and I were sifting through reams of files, I was also drafting an affidavit to conduct a Title 3 wiretap which would allow law enforcement to listen to the phone calls placed and received by ST, the president of the gang. Additionally, the lieutenant of the Milwaukee police, the captain of the Milwaukee County Sheriff's Office and I were enlisting various other agencies to help with manpower because, from prior cases, this was going to be very manpower intensive.

A wiretap involved two people monitoring the phone 24 hours a day, and a surveillance team ready to move immediately after a significant phone call. The surveillance team's duty was to validate the information received on the Title 3. That was to say that if one of the speakers on the wiretap said he was going to get a pack of cigarettes and surveillance saw him do that, the observation would validate the wiretap. An intelligence analyst was also assigned to make sense of the hundreds of daily phone calls made and received by the gang president

An example of this could be if the president of the gang called a dealer and set up a meeting with him at a certain location, the surveillance team would simply drive by that location and verify that the meeting was taking place. The best-case scenario would be if a drug transaction was set up on the wiretap, and it could

be interrupted by police without compromising the wiretap, the surveillance team would jump into action and make the arrests. Taking action on information gathered from a wiretap was always a tough call because we never wanted to jeopardize the wiretap or make the targets suspicious of their phones.

So, the affidavit was completed, approved by DEA headquarters, and the U.S. Department of Justice. Next, a federal judge read the affidavit and signed it if there was enough probable cause, which in this case was no problem. It was then time to flip the switch, which meant it was time to start listening to the conversations of the drug gang. Wags, the Assistant United States Attorney who worked with me preparing the affidavit, was in the wire room along with several agents when we started listening. The small wire room was teeming with excitement waiting to hear the first phone call which took an amazingly short period of time.

The wire room was referred to as the room where the actual recording device and listening device were placed. Within five minutes of activating the wiretap, a telephone call came in as the conversation related to trading a quarter ounce of cocaine for an Uzi submachine gun. Wags looked at me with a big grin on his face and said, "This is going to be a good one."

However, there was a problem with the wiretap during the first week or so because both the president of the gang whose phone they were listening to and anybody who called him spoke with a combination of street lingo, gang lingo and prison lingo. It was very difficult to understand, but what we usually did after a phone call was take a duplicate tape into another room that was quiet and listen to it over and over again to pick up words they couldn't understand on the original call. Because of the difficulty in understanding the conversations, we had to limit the number

of wiretap monitors, so we could familiarize themselves with the slang used by the gang.

The gang used some cryptic and colorful words or phrases. If we said," Riding deep," that meant that there were several gang members in a car while on the street getting ready for a gunfight. On one occasion, two of the principal gang members got shot, including ST's brother Michael, and when they explained it to ST, they said that the people who shot them must have been "Shorty folks" because both gang members were shot in the legs. They also referred to themselves as "folks" which simply meant that folks were part of the gang.

On many occasions the team heard the gang members discussing whether or not they had "Scotty" with them. Initially we thought that Scotty must be some kind of tough guy because there was always an ominous tone to the conversation. But later, we found out that Scotty was an AR-15, .223 caliber rifle used by the gang to intimidate or kill rivals. According to the Milwaukee Police Department and the Bureau of Alcohol and Firearms, the gang had no problem using it for intimidation or murder.

The president of the gang often received telephone calls in which he would answer, "Hit me back. I'm doing the Wild Thang." If you haven't already figured out what the wild thing is, you will in short order. When he was doing the 'wild thing' a female's voice was always in the background making, for lack of a better word, erotic noises.

What the team knew going into the wiretap from reliable sources was that when the BOS set up a drug house, they defended the turf with what became known as 'drive by shootings.' The Milwaukee Police Department and ATF estimated that in the three years prior to the wiretap, the gang was involved in approximately 40 shootings on Milwaukee's North Side. The

gang was formed after the brother of the president, Michael, was released from Statesville Prison where he was a member of the gang. After he landed in Milwaukee, he started recruiting prospects to be in the gang and also brought several of his friends from Statesville Prison to get in on the lucrative Milwaukee drug business.

ST was recruited to become the president and to obtain cocaine for his brother, the Statesville convict. Michael's job was to distribute cocaine to other gang members who put the cocaine on the streets, again typically using drug houses. The gang was doing about eight kilos of cocaine per week according to a very reliable informant. Prior to the wiretap, which I found out later, ST was losing respect on the street because of rip-offs and bad deals. Because of this, the president was becoming desperate to raise money and reestablish himself as the North Side of Milwaukee's principal cocaine distributor.

After the shooting that occurred on January 1st, 1990, when two gang members were shot in the legs by the shorty folks, things continued with the wiretap and a total of 135 hours of conversations were intercepted. Of the 135 hours of conversation, 17 hours were related to drug transactions or the conspiracy and would be introduced at trial time. One of the conversations, during which a Wisconsin Department of Justice agent and I were listening, caused quite a bit of commotion.

The president set up a deal with one of his previously known sources of supply, Debra. From the conversation it was our understanding that the president was personally going to handle the transaction to ensure that it was completed successfully. It didn't take long to decide on setting up surveillance on Debra's house. Because a surveillance team was not ready, the State Department of Justice agent and I drove out and established

surveillance at Debra's house, observing the president in very short order, parking, walking to and entering Debra's house.

Normally in situations like this, agents would consult with the U.S. attorney who would make the call as to whether or not they should take the enforcement action. Frankly, I was afraid of that because it was so early in the wiretap, that the U.S. attorney would decide not to take any enforcement action. I meant no disrespect to Wags, the Assistant U.S. Attorney in charge of the case, because it was unprecedented for an agent to take action on a wiretap without the blessings of both the boss and the attorney assigned to the case.

From listening to the gang for two weeks in a row, I was confident the gang felt immune to any police action, and as a result were arrogant and most importantly lazy. Because of that, when the president left Debra's house and started walking to his car, Bob and I started casually walking in the president's direction. At this point I was definitely ready for a huge spanking no matter what happened when the president was arrested. I was confident though that ST and his gang members were too lazy to switch out all the phones they were using. Their very lifeblood was the telephone and any interruption in telephone calls meant lost revenue.

Just before the president got into his car, he looked over his shoulder. Bob and I ran in his direction, and the president started running, but on the first or second step slipped in the grass and fell. We commanded that he stay down on the ground, spread his arms and legs and then we identified ourselves as police, not DEA agents. (The reason we didn't identify ourselves as DEA agents was because that may have caused the gang to believe they were being wiretapped.)

We then rolled the president over and when we patted him

down found a bag of cocaine in his pants. Shortly thereafter we placed him under arrest. Previously we had called the Milwaukee police and requested they provide a squad to bring the president to police headquarters. During that time, we were trying to figure out a good story to throw the president off. Before we hit the streets, I called two of my friends in the tac unit and asked them to come assist us with the arrest of the president.

When they arrived on the scene, DEA surrendered custody of the president to two 700's and told them to release him after an hour or so without providing him with any more information.

Bob and I knew that after the two 700s spent some time with the president, they would have a story that we hoped caused ST not to worry about a wiretap.

We returned to the monitor room, and it wasn't more than a half an hour or an hour after the president was released that his phone started ringing off the hook meaning the wire wasn't compromised. At about the same time Wags came into the monitor room and let me know that he wasn't happy with my decision to stop and search the president. Wags, without saying a word, stared at me as if I was dead to him; consequently, Wags probably would never work with me again. That thought weighed the most on me because my relationship with Wags was based on implicit trust and I violated that. (We released the president and didn't charge him because we still wanted more evidence off the wiretap.)

I became concerned when the first phone calls started coming in and the president warned his co-conspirators that his phone was either tapped or there was an informant in the organization. When the president said that his phone was possibly tapped, and to be careful what they were 'conversating,' it seemed like the end. I began questioning myself and wondered how I could have been so wrong in my evaluation of the gang.

What if they ditched all their phones and got new numbers? How far was the investigation set back because of one decision that could have easily been avoided if I would have followed protocol, (i.e. getting the approval of Wags and my boss. Maybe the gang wasn't as lazy as I first thought, and they were all going to get new phones based on the president's warning.)

A very short while later, I was pleasantly surprised, even ecstatic, that each time the president warned one of his fellow crooks that his phone might be tapped, conversations related to drug deals immediately followed. In fact, the conversations were so free flowing that even though I had predicted that this would occur, I was surprised at how quickly the drug chatter started on the telephone and didn't stop at all. I was guessing that they would stop talking about drugs for a couple days and then start up again.

One time, several weeks later, in an attempt to 'tickle' the wire, the team arranged a buy using an informant. The buy would be from one of the gang's enforcers. (Tickling the wire is accomplished by conducting a street operation against the target or his people and seeing what they had to say on the phone afterwards.) After the buy went down, we purposely had two Milwaukee police officers, Mike Lewandowski, aka Blondie and his partner, both legends on the North Side of Milwaukee, stop the enforcer and literally steal the money that was used for the buy from the enforcer. The Milwaukee policeman, pretending to be corrupt officers, told the enforcer that he wasn't going to get a receipt and he wasn't going to get his money back. In fact, they told him they were stealing his money. Lewandowski, when asked for a receipt, grabbed his crotch and said, "Here's your receipt." When this conversation was played during the trial, the judge, jury, marshals, U.S. attorneys and defense attorneys all shared a pretty good laugh.

232

Minutes after the alleged theft, the enforcer immediately called the president and complained about being robbed by the two police officers. He complained to the president that when he asked for a receipt, one of the officers grabbed his crotch and said, "Here's your receipt." Our attempt to tickle the wire was successful and also provided a pretty good laugh. The Milwaukee police officers who 'stole' the money were good friends of mine and had a sense of humor. They of course surrendered the money to the DEA and was later used as evidence against the enforcer. If the gang was thinking they were wiretapped, they sure didn't say so on the phone.

The wiretap continued for several weeks until enough evidence to indict and convict the defendants was gathered. After shutting the wiretap down, I attempted, with the help of many officers and agents, to transcribe all the tape conversations. This became a task that required DEA to hire a transcription company to complete the job. After they completed transcribing the 17 hours of critical conversation, I listened to every tape and verified that the transcription was accurate. It took quite some time for the transcribers to understand the jargon and in fact I sat with them and 'translated' when they first began their task.

By the second week of February the US Attorneys determined that 30 individuals would be indicted by a federal grand jury and plans were made for the arrests. Two great lieutenants from the Milwaukee Police Department put together plans for how each individual would be arrested, processed, and transported to court. The United States Marshal Service and the U.S. Parole and Probation Office were notified to expect a busy day on February 17th. A total of 75 federal, state, and local law enforcement officers were involved in the operation, each assigned a specific task and location.

Besides the 30 arrest warrants, affidavits were prepared for four search warrants to be executed along with the 30 arrests. Although the law enforcement officers that were involved in the investigation knew what was happening, nobody else was advised until the early morning hours of February 17th at which time the arrests and search warrants were executed.

Approximately one-half kilo of cocaine and $10,000 in cash along with weapons, five vehicles and other evidence were seized. At the end of the day, 24 people were arrested and delivered to the United States magistrate who set bail. Most of the defendants were denied bail by the magistrate. Consequently, many gang members had the privilege of meeting members of the United States Marshal Service for the first time.

Nothing unusual occurred during the arrest; almost all of the defendants did not resist with the exception of the president's brother, Michael. Milwaukee Police tactical officers were assigned to arrest him. He lived on the second floor with a fairly long staircase leading to the street. The brother, as I understood it, started to resist but because he was still in two leg casts from the January 1st shorty folks shooting, didn't put up much of a fight. At the bail hearing, he complained to the magistrate that the tactical squad officers grabbed him under each arm and backed him down the stairs with his legs bouncing up and down.

Although I was in the courtroom, that was the last I ever heard that story. It may have or it may not have happened. Nonetheless the magistrate ordered that I personally wheel the brother to the marshal's office which was on a different floor from the magistrate. Because of this, I had to use an elevator, and as I was backing in the elevator and pulling the wheelchair into the elevator, my attempts to make sure the brother was safe took too long, and the elevator doors kept opening and closing, crashing

against his two casted legs. If I had said that this incident was accidental, no one would have believed me.

During the next several months all of the agents, police officers and three attorneys prepared for what was going to be Milwaukee's largest criminal trial and Milwaukee's most unusual trial. A small core group of officers had essentially been working seven 10-to-12-hour days since December and although it was a grueling schedule, everybody got along and did what had to be done. I couldn't recall one argument or disagreement occurring during all the trial preparation, or for that matter during the investigation. Everybody was on exactly the same page and knew exactly what the objectives were.

Finally, during the second week of July 1990 jury selection began for the 14 gang members who used their constitutional right for a trial and their right to confront their accusers. Unfortunately for the gang, it was impossible to cross-examine a tape recording of their own voice and their own statements. Prior to the trial, the United States Marshal Service along with the presiding judge decided for the first time in the history of the Eastern District of Wisconsin, the courtroom would be closed to the public and only the marshals, the defendants, defense attorneys and interested government parties would be allowed in the courtroom. A separate room on a different floor with a taped television feed was provided for the public's viewing of the trial.

As it turned out, closing the courtroom off was indeed a wise move based on the irreverent and sometimes violent behavior of the defendants while in court. Even though the defendants were shackled by the marshals, and each defendant had two marshals sitting on either side, we never knew what to expect. The first incident occurred not long after the trial began when the gang members refused to leave a Wisconsin County Jail to attend the

trial. The presiding judge, who was not one for playing patty cakes, told the marshals to do whatever they had to do to get the defendants their due process.

As the story was relayed to me, each defendant over a period of a week or so had to be forcibly removed by the marshal's service which meant that the gang had to get up at 5 a.m. because it took until at least after 6 a.m. to get the gang all shackled up and in the transport vehicles for 7:00 o'clock trial. In addition to being upset about the early morning wake up, the gang also had to sit in court, just like everybody else, until 5 p.m. when they were returned to county jail.

The three assistant United States attorneys and I were present in court every day and were seated at the front table in front of all the gang members. Marshals and defense attorneys were seated directly behind the prosecutors and me. Ironically, the president's brother was seated directly behind me and a little bit to the right, and each time he was brought into the courtroom, the brother and I exchanged sarcastic remarks with each other. Not mean remarks, just street jabbing. It got to the point where we actually started joking with each other. During one exchange the brother told me, "You ain't bad for a white boy."

My response was, "You're not so bad for a guy with your rep!"

Because I was the case agent, it was also necessary for me to be in court during those hours to assist the three prosecutors with the presentation of their case and with the cross-examination of any potential witnesses. So, at 5 p.m. I would go to the U.S. attorney's office and spend until seven or eight in the evening helping to prepare witnesses for the next day's trial. After that, there were several occasions where I had an informant who had information that was necessary to obtain and therefore went out

and met with them. On some occasions I even did deals which turned into an awfully long day.

Several interesting things occurred during the trial, one of which was when Detective Lewandowski took the witness stand and started testifying about his participation in the investigation. (Lewandowski was one of the Milwaukee tactical officers who worked the wiretap on a daily basis.) When he took the witness stand, all 14 BOS gang members gave him the finger at the same time without attempting to hide the gesture from the judge or the jury.

Not to be outdone, Detective Lewandowski put his middle finger on his cheek, where the jury couldn't see, and returned the gesture. Another incident occurred where one of the gang members seated in the back of the courtroom, picked up a pitcher of water and threw it forward causing the rest of the gang members to stand up and shout profanities at the witness. To say the least, it was a very animated couple of minutes that none of the lawyers, judge or I had ever witnessed or experienced. The marshals were incredibly well prepared for this rebellion and got all the gang under control in minutes.

At the time of the above incident, Detective Lewandowski was on the witness stand and had a 55-gallon drum full of pistols, rifles, shotguns and automatic weapons including Sparky, right in front of the officer. The officer identified them and indicated how, when and from whom they were seized. When the courtroom erupted, I ran up to the judge and escorted him to his chambers and locked down until the marshals could settle the gang down. It took less than ten minutes or so, but order was finally restored and the trial proceeded. Each defendant's attorney had the right to cross examination which meant that

for every witness that took the stand, 14 attorneys challenged the veracity of the witness.

Finally, during the first week of August, it was my turn to take the witness stand and testify regarding the tape conversations. I testified about the content of 17 hours of recorded telephone conversations. The testimony was excruciatingly slow because the gang used so much slang that had to be explained to make sense to the jury. Each of the conversations had some kind of relationship to the gang or drug dealing. Prior to taking the witness stand, it took several months of listening to each tape several times before I could actually play a conversation all the way through without having to stop it. Most of that kind of work occurred during the evenings or weekends.

Everybody in the courtroom was provided a headset and I basically translated much of the conversations because they were all street jargon and very difficult to understand. A majority of the conversations were not for the faint of heart because of the generous use of expletives by the gang. One of the defense attorneys actually asked if I had any problem understanding the conversations that were played over a five-day stint when I was on the witness stand.

I indicated that I didn't have any problem understanding them. The attorney responded that I was probably the only one in the courtroom who could comprehend what they were saying. Another defense attorney asked if I used a translator when listening to the tapes. In today's sensitive world that question probably would never have been asked for fear of offending those viewing the trial who were faint of heart. Taking a step back, remember that the courtroom was only occupied by 14 defendants, 28 seasoned United States Marshals, three assistant

238

United States attorneys, the judge, defense attorneys and me. Nobody else.

During the last week of August testimony came to a conclusion. Closing arguments were made by the attorneys and instructions were given to the jury by the judge. As soon as court adjourned before the jury even began deliberating, I left the courtroom, got in my government car, and drove home to leave on a long-postponed fishing vacation in The Boundary Waters of Minnesota with Mel, who by then was my brother-in-law.

At that time, it was about a 12-hour drive to get up there. On the second or third day when we returned from a hard day's fishing, I got a phone call from Wags who told me that everybody was guilty of all of the most serious counts, except the president's girlfriend who was found not guilty of four counts. As a side note she was extremely pregnant during the trial, so she could have been the ringleader, and they probably would have still found her innocent due to her pregnancy.

A few months after the guilty verdicts, the gang members had to stand before the judge and be sentenced. Each gang member was sentenced to extremely long prison terms in the federal penitentiary for periods 10 years and up. One of the more interesting and likable gang members had his conviction overturned and was released from prison. Most of the rest of the gang remained in prison for 15 years or more.

After the gang trial, I was pretty much spent. Developing probable cause for a wiretap, monitoring a wiretap that literally had hundreds of calls per day, preparing for court, listening to and transcribing hundreds of telephone calls, being involved in a six-week trial as the second chair (In the federal system most of the time when there is a trial, the case agent will sit through

the trial with the prosecutor to assist with suggestions.) and still being involved in cases produced by my informants wore me out, more mentally than physically.

46

Expert Testimony

Expert witnesses were called to provide opinions and analysis related to the specific facts of the case. As opposed to a regular witness who was not able to express an opinion, the expert witness was given that latitude because of the depth of his prior experience. In the case of a drug trial, before the expert was allowed to testify, the assistant United States attorney would determine the length of time the witness has had on the job, the number of contacts he had had both working undercover and interviewing witnesses and informants, the knowledge the expert had acquired regarding drug prices, the behavior of drug dealers and how many times he had ever testified as an expert before.

The expert would explain to the jury in layman's terms, as best he could, what specific items of evidence that were not easily understandable. The defense attorney's job was to dissect the expert's testimony and on cross-examination, bring any conflicting evidence presented by the expert to the jury's attention. The underlying strength of an expert witness was to know the facts that he was testifying about to be indisputable under a microscope. Any chink in the armor of an expert witness could lead to disastrous results in the trial, so the witness had to be ready.

47

Side Job

During June of 1990, Milwaukee police detectives Tom and Al, both longtime friends of mine and incredibly good detectives, received information from an informant that several individuals had arrived in Milwaukee from New York in possession of a kilogram of cocaine. According to the informant, they rented Room 234 of a motel near the airport in Milwaukee. Upon investigating, the officers determined that the room was rented under a fictitious name with an address that was a boarded-up home. A car parked immediately outside the motel had New York license plates.

Detectives Tom and Al established surveillance on the motel and observed a Latin male later identified as Modesto Arroyo, leave the motel and drive to a different airport hotel where he remained for about two hours. After Arroyo made his fourth trip to the hotel, Milwaukee police arrested him.

Lying on the floor of Arroyo's car was the key for Room 207 of the second hotel. Milwaukee police officers responded to Room 207 and entered it to ensure there were no more suspects. With the door remaining open, the two Milwaukee police detectives observed a large brick of cocaine in plain view inside the room.

The room was secured and a search warrant was obtained for that room.

The large brick of cocaine was later found to weigh 1.177 kilos. Arroyo was arrested for possession of and conspiracy to deliver 1.177 kilos of cocaine. (1 kg = 40 ounces) The Milwaukee detectives then returned to Room 234 of the first hotel and determined that a Bienvenudo Duarte was present in the room. Discovered on Duarte's person were 3 pieces of paper that reflected large drug transactions and a pager which contained telephone numbers from New York. During that time, pagers were used by drug dealers on a routine basis to contact each other.

When the detectives questioned him, he provided them with a false address. Duarte indicated that his only visitor that day was a guy by the name of Edwin. He said that he made or received very few telephone calls and that he was in Milwaukee arranging a singing engagement. Milwaukee Police surveillance, on the contrary, observed Arroyo going to Room 234 several times.

A simultaneous investigation revealed that 100 telephone calls were placed or received in Room 234 and furthermore, Duarte claimed he was in Milwaukee to book a singing act. Duarte was unable to name any singing acts in Milwaukee. Lastly, Duarte had an altered out of state driver's license. Things weren't going well for Duarte at this point. However, he was confident that he wasn't in legal jeopardy because there was no cocaine in Room 234.

The fairly new conspiracy laws often came as a huge surprise to drug dealers involved in conspiracies. They figured if they didn't touch the drugs or possess the drugs, they would be immune from prosecution. Ignorance was bliss for the thousands of drug dealers who manipulated other people to handle and transfer drugs instead of the actual drug dealer.

☆ ☆

After the arrest of Arroyo and Duarte the detectives presented the case to the United States attorney's office because of the amount of drugs involved and the stricter sentences in federal court. I was contacted by an assistant United States attorney who was handling this prosecution who asked that me to examine the notes and provide a detailed explanation as to what they meant. There were various annotations on the piece of paper regarding the expenses Duarte incurred and sales made. A handwriting expert determined that the writing and those three pieces of paper were in fact his.

There was also an annotation of 117,000 which based on the totality of figures on the piece of paper possessed by Duarte, I determined, without question, that Duarte was responsible for selling almost 6.5 kilos of cocaine. That determination was based on a conversation I had with a senior agent from the New York field division who told me that kilograms of cocaine were selling for $20,000 per kilo in New York during the time period of Duarte's arrest.

During November 1990 a trial began in the Eastern District of Wisconsin, and I was called as an expert witness to explain the significance of the papers possessed by Duarte. One example of this was the notation on the ledgers *70 sinta a 850 hacen $59500*. I explained to the jury that the notation meant a single sale of 70 ounces of cocaine for $850 an ounce equaled $59,500.

During the summer of 1990 that price was consistent with the sale price of $850 for a multi ounce purchase in Milwaukee, whereas in New York the multi ounce purchase would be significantly cheaper. The reason for the reduced rate in New York was because the quantity of cocaine available in New York was much greater than in Milwaukee and therefore basic market forces took control of the price. It was basically supply and demand.

244

Admittedly Duarte's notes were crude and disguised but after spending a significant amount of time working on the numbers to make sense, I concluded that without a doubt the notes reflected on the three pieces of paperwork were contemporaneous with the conspiracy that Duarte and Aroyo had entered into. That was one of the arguments of the defense counsel who purported that although the notes that Duarte possessed were in fact drug notes, they could have been from another conspiracy. He further argued that the drug notes could have come from New York or some other place and did not reflect the Milwaukee transactions.

I described how drug traffickers almost always had to keep drug ledgers to remember who owed them and how much. Also, I had to describe to them how drug traffickers took larger quantities of cocaine, for example a kilogram (2.2 lbs.), and would break it down to ounces to sell to their dealers at an inflated price. Their dealers in turn would break the ounces into 28 grams which was equal to one ounce.

Then the lower-level dealers would sell single gram packages of cocaine. On each progression down the ladder from a kilo, to ounces, to grams the dealers would cut their coke to increase its bulk, weight and most importantly profit. (For cocaine a cut was typically a white-water soluble product that matched the color of cocaine which was also a white crystalline powder)

Further evidence of the numerical annotations on the three pieces of paper were the Spanish words for debt, credit and minus. Duarte was simply keeping track of how much it cost him to buy the cocaine, ($117,000) and how much he was selling, who he was selling to and what price he was charging. The price Duarte was selling the coke for was again consistent with Milwaukee prices during June of 1990. Apparently, the jury and the judge

not only understood and believed my testimony but agreed with it and convicted Duarte the same day the trial began.

During January of 1991, the judge who heard the Duarte case sentenced him to 180 months in prison. Although the original charges carried a maximum of 15 years in prison, the judge was allowed to look at the totality of the weight of cocaine Duarte dealt with. Considering my testimony regarding the interpretation of the drug notes, the judge sentenced him way above what the original charges would have called for. The defense council appealed the prison sentence arguing that the government hadn't proved that Duarte was responsible for more than five kilos of cocaine. The defense also argued that the government hadn't proved that the conspiracy actually occurred in Milwaukee.

After several hearings at the Seventh Circuit Court of Appeals, during August of 1993, it was determined that Duarte was responsible for dealing over 5 kilos of cocaine, and it was dealt in Milwaukee while in a conspiracy with Arroyo. The lengthy prison sentence imposed on Duarte was affirmed and all of the government's testimony regarding the three pieces of drug notes found in Duarte's wallet was also allowed to be considered. Arroyo was also sentenced to a significant time in federal prison.

As a side note, both Detective Al and Detective Tom could have easily been qualified as experts in the drug field. As expert testimony evolved in drug cases, it became apparent that a better expert witness would be one who has no skin in the game and could be completely impartial. Although I testified as an expert in many of my own cases, the circuit courts began challenging the impartiality of the agent who was both the case agent and the expert witness. The United States attorney's office pivoted and started using experts who had nothing at all to do with the case in order to prevent unnecessary appeals.

48

A New Technique and Two New Partners

In 1988 I met and befriended a Milwaukee police detective by the name of Oscar Perez, who was assigned to Milwaukee's narcotic squad. Oscar frequently came over to the DEA office where we would have a cup of coffee and talk about the drug situation in Milwaukee. Over a period of several months we developed a list of potential targets in the Milwaukee drug trafficking scene. In fact the list was so long that it would be impractical to go after all of them using traditional investigative techniques. I suggested to Oscar and he enthusiastically embraced the idea of going to a targets house, "introducing" ourselves as police and telling the target we were going to work at putting him in jail.

We approached this new technique, conservatively and cautiously, but soon were amazed at how a simple knock on the door and introduction sometimes led to a successful consent. More drugs, money or weapons were found the longer we worked on the new investigative technique. The more successful we got, and in pretty short order, we began having more successes than failures. Although the new technique was producing enough,

both of us in 1989 were distracted by bigger projects. For me it was the Milwaukee straight street gang and for Oscar it was a case that we both started, but Oscar finished, involving the Marielito Cubans, many of whom settled in Wisconsin and we're dealing large quantities of cocaine.

When Oscar finally finished the Cuban case he had arrested at least 22 Cubans, seized almost $1 million in cash and during a number of different operations 44 kg of cocaine. This whole case started with a simple knock on the door and an introduction by detective Perez and myself to a Cuban, who pointed us in the right direction after our partnership ended. Fortunately, our friendship endured.

The Oak Creek Police Department assigned a veteran officer to our DEA task force who had over 20 years of experience during late 1990 or early 1991. After a couple of weeks with DEA, I bonded with the officer, Sharky. Not only did we work well together and complement each other, but we also became friends. Our wives also became friends, and we have maintained our friendships.

As mentioned earlier, I conducted a training program in Thailand. While off duty I went to a street market and purchased a number of items including a small metallic pig which the vendor indicated would provide me with good luck. I took the pig back to Milwaukee and put it on my desk, telling the guys in the office that if they needed luck when they went out on the street, all they had to do was touch the 'Magic Pig' and they would have luck. After Sharky and I teamed up, it became tradition to touch the Magic Pig before we went on the street for any type of deal.

While I worked in Milwaukee, I noticed that many loads of drugs were being delivered to Milwaukee's South Side late in the week, and that the drivers from Texas or Chicago would

generally stay the weekend, get drunk, and then head back to Texas or Chicago for another load early the next week. I also reflected on the many occasions when I went to the door of a possible witness or a suspect I needed to question, I was almost always let in by the suspect. The success of gaining entrance to the suspects' or witnesses' residences rested almost exclusively on the initial non-confrontational and polite manner I used when first introducing myself.

After Oscar left, Sharky, the Oak Creek police officer assigned to the DEA task force, and I decided that it would be a good strategy to drive by the residences of known drug dealers on Monday mornings to see if any cars with Texas, Florida, or Illinois license plates were parked nearby. On some occasions we would just go to the home of a known drug dealer, knock on the door, and ask permission to enter the residence to question the occupant about suspected drug trafficking.

This approach of contacting a suspected drug dealer was contrary to everything taught about drug investigations during this time period. Ninety-five per cent of enforcement activities on drug-related crimes were conducted as quietly as possible, and the last thing agents wanted to do was to let the suspect know he was under investigation. Our reasoning for knocking on the door and introducing ourselves to the suspect was that there was simply nothing to lose. The dealers already assumed they were under investigation. It also didn't hurt because the success of Shark and I had allowed us to miss the Monday morning staff meetings which were always boring and didn't add much to the game.

Before we started doing our Monday morning drive-bys, we discussed some basic ground rules that would have to be observed in the event we seized evidence and wanted to prosecute. We

mostly relied on our many years of experience testifying in court, sitting through trials, training, and actual search and seizure events which taught us what we had to be careful of in order to prevent tainting a potential search with a violation of the Fourth Amendment.

Surprisingly, a strong cross examination by a skilled defense attorney was one of the best tools to use as a guideline. Both Sharky and I had hundreds of cross-examinations to refer to in order to walk around landmines when talking to potential defendants. Basically Sharky and I were just fine-tuning the technique detective Oscar Perez and I used when "introducing" ourselves.

We always knocked on the front door, tried to be as non-threatening as possible when the door was answered, spoke softly, and when admitted allowed the suspect to pick the spot for the conversation. (within reason) We also told the suspect that he retained the right to ask the agents to leave at any time and if the suspect felt uncomfortable about answering a question, made it clear that he did not have to answer. We used the words "could" and "please" often in attempting to put the suspects at ease.

In almost every case when we were allowed into the house or apartment, some kind of illegal drugs or guns were found lying in plain view. If that were the case, we purposely did not react to the observation and pretended to have not made the observation. Sometimes however if a weapon was involved, we were forced to seize it in case there was somebody else in the house. After the seizure of the weapon, we would downplay its ultimate importance in a drug case and try to keep the suspect off guard.

49

Monday Morning Texas Car

Our first activity related to the new technique, later referred to as the knock and talk, occurred when we drove by a home occupied by known drug traffickers on South 11th Street. Both Sharky and I noticed that on the same side of the street as the drug dealer's home a car from Texas was parked with one car parked directly north of it and another one directly south.

The strange thing was that both the north parked car and the south parked car were touching bumpers with the Texas car which would prevent it from driving away. Because the Texas car was parked almost adjacent to the suspects that we were going to question, we both assumed (knew) that the Texas car was a load car.

Sharky and I double parked and inspected the inside of the Texas car and saw some packages lying on the floor in the backseat area. On a whim, I sniffed the outside of the trunk area and bingo, I could clearly smell marijuana. I noted at the time that it was a windy day, and it was coming from the north which helped push the smell of the marijuana through the crack of the trunk. It wasn't a very difficult decision to maintain surveillance of that vehicle and see who entered it. I also recalled at the time

of the above sniff that some court made a ruling that stated, "The Nose Knows."

It didn't take long when we observed a Latin man leave a house on the other side of the street and walk to and attempt to enter the car that was blocked in. As soon as he stuck the keys in the door lock, we left our car and approached the Latin male. The irony of the above was that the Latin male came from a house that was previously unknown to DEA and certainly not the house of the suspects we were looking for. It was fair to point out that this incident occurred about an hour and a half before the Monday morning meeting, and that we had no intention of missing it.

It was also completely logical to assume that the Latin male was getting in the car not to drive away but to retrieve drugs, cash, or a weapon or all of the above. When we began talking to him, he broke out in a sweat and pretended that he didn't understand English. I had established probable cause to search the vehicle based on the sniff of the trunk and asked the Latin male if I could have his car keys.

He readily handed them over, and Shark popped the trunk and saw a fairly large amount of marijuana, about 150 pounds. When the passenger compartment of the car was opened, we didn't see anything suspicious. In the rear compartment of the car the packages we had previously seen were opened, and Shark discovered a pistol, a kilogram of cocaine, and a large amount of U.S. currency, about $40,000.

When Shark verbalized his find, I drew my weapon, did a quick pat down and cuffed the bad guy. At the same time this activity was occurring, both we instinctively scanned the whole area surrounding the car for other suspects who may have been coming to the aid of their compadre. If there might have been any desire on the suspects' friends to come to his aid, it quickly

evaporated when they realized Shark and I were the police.

After placing the Latin male under arrest, we turned him over to the United States Marshals in Milwaukee who determined that he was wanted on a federal fugitive warrant out of Texas. We processed all of the evidence as we routinely did and then waited for either a preliminary hearing to determine if there was probable cause for the arrest and search or if we could get to the grand jury for an indictment prior to that. The probable cause hearing came up and just before I took the witness stand, Sharky wished me good luck because neither he nor I had ever developed probable cause with our noses.

I took the witness stand before the magistrate and the Eastern District of Wisconsin and went through direct examination which was just basically a repetition of what occurred that Monday morning on South 11th Street. The defense attorney was somewhat aggressive trying to attack my credibility regarding whether I really smelled the marijuana. I was firm in my testimony, and ultimately the magistrate indicated that there was probable cause for the search and that there was actually legal precedent to support the findings of my sniff of the trunk. The defendant was remanded to jail and returned to Texas to face his original charges. The defendant went to jail for a long time.

There are numerous Supreme Court cases that refer to the ability of a canine's nose to recognize drugs when sniffed. That sniff for sure was beneficial to both the government for the seizures, the capture of a federal fugitive and subsequent successful prosecution. It was also beneficial to Sharky and me because we missed a Monday morning meeting.

50

Another Monday Morning Meeting Missed

So, The Shark and I continued our pursuit on Monday mornings based on an illogical number of successes. On this particular Monday morning, a marijuana trafficker's house, again located in Milwaukee's South Side, had a car parked in front of it with Texas plates. The time was about 9 a.m., which ironically was about the time the Monday morning meeting began, again without us! We decided to knock on the door and see if we could get some questions answered regarding the Texas car.

As we approached the house, Sharky knocked on the door and we heard some scurrying within. The door was answered by a Latin male. He became extremely nervous and began sweating profusely during our introduction. BINGO!!!! He let us inside the house, and we told him we were suspicious of the Texas car and wondered if he knew anything about it.

He very quickly asked me to follow him into the basement while Sharky stood guard at the front door. He was moving so quickly I was actually concerned he may be going for a gun. When I descended into the basement, the Latin male said he didn't want to be any part of shooting a policeman. He continued stating that

when we knocked on the door, the man who drove the Texas car had climbed into the attic, was armed and indicated he would shoot without hesitation. It goes without saying that a number of decisions had to be made and made quickly.

The first was to pat down the guy I was with because there wasn't enough time from entering the house to hitting in the basement. Next, I had to get upstairs and alert Sharky who was calmly standing at the doorway awaiting my return. The last thing was to get more help and get it quickly. I radioed the DEA office who were all congregated in a meeting and briefly spoke to the Resident Agent in Charge.

I requested that the Resident Agent in Charge contact the Tactical Unit, 700s, brief them quickly and have them join us. While I was talking to the RAIC, Sharky was pointing his weapon at the door leading to the attic. Several other people were in the house including children who I escorted out while Sharky kept the gun on the attic door.

It wasn't more than five or six minutes when we heard the sirens of the approaching tactical units, definitely a pleasant sound. Upon their arrival, the sergeant who at one time butted heads with me, got a quick briefing, assembled the rest of the tac squad, and they entered the house. Before making the entry, DeValkanaere, one of my buddies on the 700-team looked over his shoulder and said, "the men will take it from here". Sharky and I, who remained outside, heard muffled noises from inside the house where the Tac Squad guys barked commands at the hidden suspect.

After just a few minutes, the word "clear" could be heard coming from the house meaning everything was safe and the bad guy was in cuffs. The initial Latin male who answered the door revealed the location of a big stack of marijuana which was seized

along with the car that had the Texas plates. The marijuana was wrapped in plastic and then duct tape and each package weighed about 2.2 pounds.

The Texas dealer was prosecuted in state court and ended up with a minor prison sentence. This was an instance that could have exploded into violence in about a New York minute had the bad guy in the attic begun shooting. The women and children in the house were the only things preventing him from pulling the trigger.

51

Another Bingo

Within a week or two of the above incidents, Sharky and I were doing our Monday morning spot checks when we discovered a car parked in front of a well-known cocaine trafficker's house that we had not seen during prior surveillances. Ironically the time was about 8 a.m., and the office meeting would convene in an hour. We decided to knock on the door to see if we could ask some questions about the car, so we parked our official government vehicle and knocked on the door.

The guy who answered spoke decent English, so I explained to him that I was suspicious of the car parked in front of his house, and if he'd be willing to let us in to answer some questions. He agreed that we could come in, but he would only talk to me for some reason while Sharky remained inside the threshold of the door. His refusal to talk to Sharky was based on the reputation The Shark had on Milwaukee South Side. Several informants had spoken to us about the DEA agent *El Tiburon* and the fear he instilled in the dope dealers not only because of his size but because of the reputation he was earning—Quiet but deadly!

The guy who answered the door walked me to a kitchen table where I could see the Shark standing at the entryway but inside

the house. I was explaining his rights to the occupant of the house and the fact that he didn't have to answer any questions. He was very cooperative and said he would answer any questions. I began with the basics, asking him his name and if he lived there, etc.

After gathering some background information, I glanced up and saw Sharky lip syncing the word "trouble." I paused the interview and asked if I could be excused for a second to talk to my partner. Not knowing what the trouble was, I prepared myself for any possibility slowly raising my right hand up my leg toward my weapon trying not to be too obvious. As usual *El Tiburon* was calm as a cucumber.

I left the kitchen table and walked about 15 feet to where Shark was stationed. When I got close enough, Shark shot his eyes in a very obvious manner to the left. With that, I glanced slightly to my right and saw on a coffee table not 10 feet from Shark several decent sized bags of cocaine and a pistol. We did not tip our hand at this point, but the time was coming. I knew that Shark would have my back as well as covering the room that contained the drugs and the weapon.

I returned to the kitchen table and asked, "Are there any other occupants of the house?"

"No," was the response. I then asked if there were any drugs, guns or money in the house and he indicated that there was not. For the second time I made sure that he was aware of his rights, and when he indicated he was, I placed him under arrest while Sharky simultaneously seized the pistol and cocaine which was about a half a kilogram. While I was making the arrest, Sharky was clearing the rest of the house. Neither of the us had to say a word to each other but just acted out of instinct.

When we arrived at the office with the defendant and the evidence, one of the Waukesha County sheriff deputies assigned

to the DEA task force looked at me and sarcastically said, "Another good knock and talk." It was funny because on Monday mornings most of the guys when asked where The Shark and I were, would say that they were just doing a Monday morning knock and talk. This was not to be confused with 'knock and Announce' which was a totally different tactic mostly used on search or arrest warrants.

Because we were so well known on the south side streets, we decided to just park our OGV and walk up and down streets that were well known as hotbeds of drug activity. Believe it or not, on several occasions grandmotherly type women would invite us into their homes for breakfast, which was always amazing and involved chorizo and eggs nearly all the time!

During breakfast the women would often mention that such and such house had unusual activity going on, and we should be aware of it. I found it very satisfying that of the 30 or 40 walks that The Shark and Will took in gang and drug dealer turf, we were never once confronted by criminals. I believed the reason for this was simply because there was a respect for law enforcement authorities back then.

Since that era, politicians and district attorneys became more concerned with idealistic dreams rather than realism. I also believed that when we were doing the walking, a lot of toilets were being flushed with drugs, and a lot of leases were being broken because nobody wanted to live in a neighborhood where DEA agents were on foot patrol.

52

Just Another Monday

The next week the action actually began on Sunday. On a Sunday evening while at home, I received a call from an informant who told me that a very well-known drug trafficker had just returned from Chicago and had stashed two kilos of cocaine in the engine compartment of his car. The informant further provided me with a description of the make and model of the vehicle and told me that it was parked right across the street from the trafficker's house.

This of course provided me with the opportunity to avoid the Monday morning meeting. Sharky and I met, went to the drug trafficker's home, and knocked on the door. After several knocks, Sharky blurted out, "Beto, its Sharky. Open up." Because of prior contacts Sharky and I had with the trafficker, we knew him, and he knew us.

The trafficker's demeanor was not consistent with past contacts we had with him, and he was clearly agitated and nervous. Attempts to settle him down a little bit were met with little success. After watching the dealer sweat for three or four minutes *El Tiburon* abandoned his calm behavior and opted for a little more aggressive approach. I always enjoyed the aggressive Sharky because it was so out of character and a complete act, maybe.

Sharky pointed to the suspect's car that allegedly contained two kilos of cocaine and asked Beto if he knew whose car that was. Of course the trafficker denied that the car was his. I then asked the trafficker if he had any car keys in his pocket to which he responded that he did. I asked him to remove the keys so I could see them. At this point he handed the keys to me. He was shaking like a wire in a high wind. Although I felt we had probable cause to search the car without a warrant, we asked and received permission from Beto to search the car. Of course, he had keys which matched the make and model of the vehicle the informant described.

I took the car keys, walked across the street and opened the car. Beto indicated that he must have accidentally picked those keys up from a bar the night before, and he didn't know whose keys they were. Shark and I searched the passenger compartment of the car first as a ruse to throw the trafficker off. After completing the search of the passenger compartment without any evidence, Sharky and I purposely walked to the front of the car directing Beto to join them.

Accompanying us, the drug dealer engaged in a conversation about which bar the drug dealer was in the night before. In the middle of that conversation Sharky said, "Hey, before we leave, let's check under the hood and the trunk." After checking the trunk without any results, we popped the hood and sitting as plain as day in a black plastic bag were two kilos of cocaine. We arrested the trafficker, seized the drugs and transported both the trafficker and the drugs to the Milwaukee office. On a later date, just as with all the above cases, Beto pleaded guilty of possession with intent to distribute and was sentenced to prison.

The knock and talks and the Monday morning drive bys were not typical DEA investigations. They began as a result of

☆ ☆

my being burnt out, having a new partner and looking for a novel approach. Although I didn't expect the success that we had, I was happy to do something a little bit differently and still have an impact on the community.

Many more arrests and seizures occurred, but unfortunately time erased many significant parts of those actions. A new investigative tool seemed to have evolved out of the knock and talk. For sure, as I indicated above, we took some dope off the streets as well as the dope dealers. Although I couldn't say for sure, but plenty of drugs were probably destroyed to get rid of the evidence when Sharky and I were patrolling the South Side.

53

One Last Milwaukee Conversation

It became time in my career to move on, so I applied for a supervisor's position in New Orleans and was accepted for it. But *Tiburon* and I weren't done yet and had one more interview we wanted to conduct. It was with the president of a prominent South Side gang who had been responsible for all kinds of mischief including allegations of murders and drug trafficking. We knew that he worked in a factory and generally got off of work at 4 o'clock. So about 3:30 *Tiburon* and I established surveillance on his house and saw a couple kids playing in his yard on a swing set along with a woman we suspected to be his wife.

After his wife and kids went inside the house, Sharky sat on a picnic table in his yard, and I sat in a swing, swinging back and forth. The president's wife must have called him at the factory because it wasn't more than 10 minutes after we entered his yard when he drove up and confronted us. After we told him we were DEA agents, he looked at Sharky and said, "Oh, you must be *El Tiburon*." That happened all the time when Sharky and I made our first approaches, leaving me to think I must be chopped liver because nobody ever told me I must be *El Tiburon*. But the truth

of the matter was that there was absolutely no competition or envy between us two partners because we literally worked as one.

After some more conversation, Sharky told him that he and I were going to dedicate the next several months investigating the leader in an attempt to put him in jail for the rest of his life. There was much more conversation, but in the end, he asked if Sharky had a business card with a phone number and Sharky replied, "*Tiburon* will do."

After the above meeting, I transferred to New Orleans. I had forgotten about that encounter only because I was busy acclimating to my new position as a group supervisor. A month or two later, Sharky called me up to tell me that he had been contacted by a prominent Milwaukee attorney who was a longtime acquaintance of mine an adversary and friend. Sharky told me that the gang leader had contacted the attorney whose advice was to cooperate which he in fact did and developed several successful cases in the Milwaukee area.

54

Another Airplane Ride

As I talked about earlier, during the middle to late 1980s and into the 1990s, I was continually looking for a new way to get the adrenaline pumping. One of the escapes was calling a couple friends who worked at the DEA Chicago Air Wing and have them fly up to Milwaukee, pick me up, and then conduct surveillance on potential targets. Generally, all I would need during one of these surveillances would be one surveillance vehicle to check addresses that the target stopped at or people who met the guy I was watching from 2,000 feet up.

One specific surveillance happened when Sharky had an informant who told him about a Leonel Ruiz in Waukegan, Illinois, who was about to deliver a large quantity of cocaine in Milwaukee. The informant further advised that Ruiz would leave his home in Waukegan and drive to a farm in Kenosha County where he would pick up the cocaine. On the given day, a surveillance was established in Waukegan on Ruiz's red vehicle both on the ground and with me in the air. At about the time the informant said Ruiz would be heading to the farmhouse, I saw him enter his car and start heading north.

I maintained visual contact on the red car while the rest of the surveillance units remained about a half a mile or so behind

so as not to be seen by Ruiz. I watched him as he drove to Kenosha and pulled into the driveway of a farmhouse located off I-94. I saw Ruiz park his car, walk to, and enter the farmhouse. A few minutes later I saw Ruiz move his car to an outbuilding where he was joined by one more individual, who of course I could not identify because we were several thousand feet above.

Shortly after observing the second individual, I saw a black pickup truck leave the farm and start heading north on I-94 towards Milwaukee. Sharky had previously talked with the Milwaukee County Sheriff's Department to have two deputies parked on the Milwaukee County Line and I-94 and when given the signal they would pull the black pickup truck over and attempt to determine if there was cocaine present. As the black pickup truck approached Milwaukee County, the deputies turned on their red lights and pulled the vehicle over. The Milwaukee County Sheriff's Department was used to this procedure in order to protect the identity of the informant and make the drug dealers think that this was just a traffic stop.

We were in radio contact with the deputies who shortly after the stop advised that they had recovered a 12-pack size box with three kilos of cocaine in it. A guy later identified as Ramon Navarro and Ruiz were arrested and transported to the Milwaukee office of DEA. As the deputies stopped the black pickup truck, I was dropped off at the Milwaukee airport, picked up my official government vehicle and drove to the Milwaukee office, awaiting the arrival of the rest of the surveillance agents and the two prisoners.

After Sharky and I arrived at the Milwaukee DEA office, we advised Navarro of his rights and obtained a consent to search his farmhouse. We started questioning Navarro who blamed

everything on Ruiz. Because he was blaming everything on Ruiz, I told him that he didn't have anything to worry about if he was innocent, and that it was not DEA's business to put innocent people in jail. When questioned about the box of cocaine, he denied having any knowledge of the box or of the cocaine. I told him if that were the case, he would probably be innocent. Before that occurred, Sharky was going to submit the box for a fingerprint examination which would prove his innocence.

At that point his story changed somewhat when he indicated that, oh yeah, he did remember Ruiz handing him the box and asking him to place it in the car. He also told several other lies that were totally inconsistent with what had been observed by law enforcement. So, Sharky and I transported both Navarro and Ruiz to jail and then proceeded down to Kenosha to search the farm. Navarro had previously stated that DEA would find nothing in the farm because he wasn't involved in this drug transaction.

When we arrived at the farm and searched it, we found an ounce of cocaine, $5,000 in cash in between the mattress and the box spring, and plastic baggies with their corners cut which was typical of baggies used by drug dealers. Further search of Navarro's truck also revealed a bottle of inositol, a very common agent used to cut the cocaine in order to increase the quantity of cocaine and of course to increase profit.

Ruiz's car which remained in the parking lot of Navarro's farmhouse was searched and found to contain a trap compartment typically used to conceal cocaine when in transit. Ruiz's house was searched in Waukegan and a .9 mm handgun with obliterated serial numbers was found. The search was conducted on Ruiz's house because when questioned, he indicated that he left to drive to Kenosha from a location other than his house. Of course, he was observed by DEA leaving his house.

☆ ☆

During February of 1995, the trial for Navarro and Ruiz began, and a couple days later they were found guilty of both counts of possession with intent and conspiracy. Interestingly, during the trial Sharky developed two witnesses who indicated that Ruiz had transported two to four kilograms of cocaine per week to Milwaukee during a period of about three years. They also indicated that Ruiz was always armed when they conducted cocaine transactions with him. In the end, Ruiz was sentenced to many years in prison. Navarro was sent to prison but for a much shorter length of time.

55

New Orleans

During 1995, Jeanne and I transferred to New Orleans where we spent the next five years. During that time, Jeanne was making buys of crack cocaine off the most unsavory characters one could imagine. She then became the public information officer for the New Orleans Field Division and then was promoted to the RAIC of the Gulfport DEA office. She became a supervisor and established herself as an excellent one. At any given time, she was in charge of 10 to 15 male agents whose respect she gained in very short order.

On the other hand, I received a promotion upon transferring to New Orleans and my first assignment was supervising a REDRUM Group. (Spell REDRUM backwards!) We were charged with identifying and investigating drug related homicides. Next, I was assigned to a metropolitan enforcement team whose job was to go to hot spots in various parts of the state to put the drug dealers in jail. My last assignment in New Orleans was to be in charge of a group of FBI agents, U.S. Customs, DEA agents and New Orleans police officers during which time we either ran or assisted with running 10 to 15 Title 3 investigations–Wiretaps.

My career came to a screeching halt during an arrest when a New Orleans policeman and I arrested a 20-year-old guy high

on crack. He resisted, ran, and during the chase I became more of a liability to the police officer than an asset. The police officer caught the bad guy, but I came up to assist way too late. It was time for me to go 10/7, out of service.

56

Strike Three

During the early 2000's the Old Ranger and I both retired, Old Ranger living in Charleston, North Carolina, and I in Wisconsin. The phone calls continued between us two as did the jabs and of course the reminiscing. Both of us were running out of friends from the old days that we could call and harass. One night while Jeanne was relaxing after work and I was having a cold one, the phone rang, and Jeanne answered.

It was the Old Ranger's stepson, who I met while in D.C. and was staying at the Old Ranger's home as a guest. I was attending Trauma Team training. Watching the color drain from Jeanne's face meant that this was not a good call. Neither Jeanne nor I had ever talked to the stepson independent of the Old Ranger or his wife.

I listened in and heard the stepson explain that the Old Ranger had suddenly died in his beloved home office in Charleston. The conversation continued for a few more minutes with the stepson providing as much information as he had available. Of course, the Old Ranger's wife was not yet able to speak about it but said she would call when she had gathered the strength.

A week or two later my sister Donna, received a call from the Old Ranger's wife. They had become close friends over the

☆ ☆

years as a result of the friendships forged between Mel, myself, and the old Ranger. Donna learned that the Old Ranger died in his favorite chair, suffering a massive heart attack. Several weeks later a memorial was held in Springfield, Illinois, of course at the Fraternal Order of Police chapter. I said a few words bidding farewell to a good friend and fellow agent.

57

The Transition

After I retired, I sat back and fished and golfed and met some new friends with a completely different lifestyle. I worked a half a dozen part-time jobs including cutting grass at the golf course, delivering pharmaceutical drugs to drug stores for a delivery service, delivering meals on wheels, and several others, the most significant of which was conducting background checks on military personnel. I always appreciated the work that the military did, but after interviewing hundreds of soldiers, including privates and colonels, I really came to appreciate how lucky America was because of the selfless individuals that made the United States the greatest country in the world.

One night while watching a police television show, I heard one of the actors say that he was going to go out with his partner and do a knock and talk. I looked at my wife, and we both just kind of said "hmmm." Over the next several years, I heard that term repeated many times on various police shows, and each time questioned whether the technique that Oscar Shark and I had used back in the early 90s may have spread beyond Milwaukee. The icing on the cake was when I saw a news article about a couple of federal agents being prevented by a supervisor from doing a knock and talk on a prominent political figure. More recently, an

article was written about ICE using the knock and talk as one of their primary enforcement tools for immigration enforcement.

That piqued my curiosity and led me to the internet where I discovered that the knock and talk had been the subject of hundreds of state and federal court decisions. Much to my surprise, the knock and talk had been adopted by police agencies and federal agencies throughout the country as standard operating procedure. Some major police departments actually had knock and talk squads that executed them the way Oscar, Sharky and I did. Everything that I could find regarding knock and talks occurred several years after Oscar, Sharky and I began using them.

I did find two mentions of knock and talks which occurred in the late 1980s, preceding our experiment. Those mentions appeared in a book written by a DEA agent and in a Florida appeals court decision many years after the South Side of Milwaukee knock and talks. Both mentions referred to singular events rather than an enforcement strategy. By that time the term 'knock and talk' had become common parlance in the law enforcement community and the references to them were retrospective.

Law professors from several prestigious universities wrote articles about the legality of the technique. A legal analysis of the technique was written in the FBI law enforcement Bulletin. The definition of a knock and talk shows up in Wikipedia, and many law firms throughout the United States have written articles concerning the different aspects of the knock and talk. Several United States Courts of Appeals examined various knock and talks and whether they were conducted properly by the officers or agents. The appeals courts generally looked favorably upon what eventually was called the Knock and Talk Doctrine.

The Supreme Court of the United States issued a ruling that indicated there was an implicit license that permitted a visitor to approach a home by the front door, knock and after a reasonable amount of time leave if nobody answered the door. The Supreme Court noted that a police officer not armed with a warrant may approach a home and knock, precisely because that is no more than what a private citizen might do.

Of all the knock and talks Oscar, Sharky and I conducted that resulted in criminal charges, any motions to suppress the evidence seized were handled at the federal magistrate level, and the searches and seizures were all found to be constitutional. I was unable to locate any of our cases that went to the Seventh Circuit Court of Appeals. I don't think I'll ever know the answer to whether or not Oscar Sharky and I were the first ones to do a drug knock and talk but they were a great tool.

About the Author

Agent Hehr is a graduate of the University of Illinois Chicago campus and began his career with DEA's predecessor agency, the Bureau of Narcotics and Dangerous Drugs in 1972. Bill spent 28 years as a special agent working in the Chicago, Milwaukee and New Orleans offices. During that time he spent 23 years working undercover on hundreds of cases which resulted in the dismantling of high-level drug trafficking organizations. In addition, he participated in hundreds of high-risk drug-related search warrants from the inner cities of Chicago to the projects of New Orleans. Bill was qualified as an expert drug witness and testified in over 50 trials. He was one of the first, if not the first, law enforcement officer to conduct the "knock and talk" investigation which has been used as an investigative technique by local, state and federal agencies throughout the United States. During the course of his career he was a member of the Chicago Division Training team and taught thousands of Narcotics investigators throughout the United States and internationally, undercover techniques, informant handling and surveillance techniques. During his career he received numerous awards and commendations from The Drug Enforcement Administration, the Wisconsin Narcotics Officers Association, the Internal Revenue Service, the US Department of Justice and the Louisiana State Police. When Bill transferred to New Orleans, the Mayor of Milwaukee presented him with a plaque commemorating that day as Bill Hehr Day.